ST PETERSBURG

POCKET GUIDE

G000039789

STON

Charcoal Broiled STEAKS

●100 m

ER POT

DIAMANT
Restaurant

BROOKLAWN

●100 m

JOE'S BURGERS
Restaurant

ARTS & CULTURE

Space disco
featuring th

A TO Z INFO

SHOPPIN

Shopping
around
be fi

GATE BRIDGE

● MAP

LIKE   SHARE

Sailing under the Golden Gate Bridge
today, it is interesting to consider that
engineers once thought it impossible to
span the Golden Gate Strait at this point,
because of the depth of the water (318ft/
97 meters, at its deepest point) and the
powerful tidal rush.

The city authorized studies for a bridge
in 1917, but it was 1933 before the first
shovel turned under the gaze of master
engineer Joseph B. Strauss (no relation
to the famous waltz composer). Four
years later the bridge opened, at a cost
of $35 million and the lives of 11
construction workers. Today the bridge

INSIGHT ⊙ GUIDES
SPAIN

☰   INTRODUCTION

EXPLORE

Q

ILABLE $8.00

FLORIDA
This new edition of Insight Guide
Florida is a comprehensive full-colour
travel guide packed with inspiration
and information. It includes everything
from colourful surf, Wars and...

FRANCE
The brand new edition Insight Guide
to France features outstanding
full-colour photography, with this
edition containing... our brand new
photographic guide to our entire
explorations of all the places to go...

$8.00

$8.00

FRANCE

LUCIA Pocket Guide
This is one of the most luxurious
islands, prone to dramatic
beaches and a thrifty
guide... Pocket Guide, st
guide.

$8.00

Walking Eye
mobile app

Discover the world's best destinations with the Insight Guides Walking Eye app, available to download for free in the App Store and Google Play.

The container app provides easy access to fantastic free content on events and activities taking place in your current location or chosen destination, with the possibility of booking, as well as the regularly-updated Insight Guides travel blog: Inspire Me. In addition, you can purchase curated, premium destination guides through the app, which feature local highlights, hotel, bar, restaurant and shopping listings, an A to Z of practical information and more. Or purchase and download Insight Guides eBooks straight to your device.

TOP 10 ATTRACTIONS

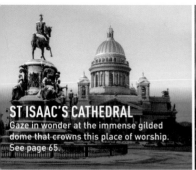

ST ISAAC'S CATHEDRAL
Gaze in wonder at the immense gilded dome that crowns this place of worship. See page 65.

PETER AND PAUL FORTRESS
Visit the original fortress where Peter the Great founded the city. See page 28.

CHURCH OF THE RESURRECTION OF CHRIST 'ON SPILLED BLOOD'
Its beautiful coloured domes are reminiscent of medieval Moscow. See page 56.

RUSSIAN MUSEUM
Home to one of the largest collections of Russian art in the world. See page 54.

PETERHOF
See the magnificent Grand Cascade fountain at the 'Russian Versailles'. See page 78.

MUSEUM OF ANTHROPOLOGY AND ETHNOGRAPHY
Peter the Great's fascinating collection of weird and wonderful medical specimens. See page 38.

WINTER PALACE AND HERMITAGE
A vast treasure trove of art collected over centuries by the Russian royal family. See page 44.

PISKARYOVSKOE CEMETERY
A sombre memorial to the victims of the blockade. See page 75.

MUSEUM OF ST PETERSBURG'S HISTORY
Find out what life was like during the blockade at this informative museum. See page 64.

YUSUPOV PALACE
The lavish interior is preserved exactly as it was when the wealthy Yusupovs lived here. See page 67.

A PERFECT DAY

9.00am

Breakfast

If you've come to Russia's north during winter, you'll need a hearty Slavic breakfast of porridge, bliny and coffee to start the day, either supplied by your hotel or from Abrikosov Café on Nevsky prospekt. In the summer, sit outside at any café or bakery on Nevsky prospekt for a bit of St Petersburger-watching.

10.00am

Palace Square

The best place to start the day is the city's epicentre, regal Dvortsovaya pl (Palace Square). The Hermitage, one of the world's greatest museums, dominates the entire northwestern flank. Soak up the square's atmosphere, but you will need to make a return visit for the Hermitage, as it takes a day or two to explore.

11.00am

Classic temple

It's a short walk from Palace Square to Isaakievskaya Square, where the neo-Classical symmetry of St Isaac's Cathedral catches the eye. Enter to admire its intricately adorned interior.

Midday

Lunch break

If you don't fancy wandering far from Isaakievskaya Square for lunch, head for La Russ on nearby nab. Reki Moiki for some classic Russian dishes.

IN ST PETERSBURG

4.30pm

Canal-hopping
End your afternoon on Nevsky prospekt where it crosses nab. Reki Fontanki, and take to the water on a boat tour. There are plenty of Russian-language tours, but Anglotourismo (www.anglotourismo.com) provide commentary in English. Catch the 5pm tour, which takes 1.5 hours.

2.00pm

Prospekt
It's time to hit St Petersburg's main street, thundering Nevsky prospect, for a spot of anything you fancy – high-end shopping, architecture gazing or simply wandering along one of Russia's most famous and intriguing thoroughfares. On your way east you will cross Zelyony and Kazansky bridges, which traverse two of the city's many canals.

9.00pm

Nightlife
What you do in the evening in St Petersburg depends on the time of year. The days of summer never end, making the white nights an excuse to party round the clock. The bitter northern winters see locals get cosy in bars and clubs, warming the cockles with shots of Russia's famous vodka, before braving the ice to the nearest metro station.

7.00pm

Teplo dinner
St Petersburg has a restaurant to suit every taste and budget, but for a real treat, head to Teplo, the nearest you might come in Russia to eating in the welcoming atmosphere of a local's home. If you are really feeling flush, book a table at Russian Empire, one of the world's finest restaurants, with prices and service to match.

CONTENTS

INTRODUCTION

After nearly a century of destruction and neglect, St Petersburg is once again emerging as Russia's most beautiful city. Founded by Peter the Great in 1703 on the marshy banks of the Neva river, the city was built as a 'window onto Europe' and as the modern successor to the old capital of Moscow. Built on 44 islands set among canals and rivers and traversed by more than 300 bridges, it is a city where pastel-coloured palaces are reflected in the canals, where mansions and churches harmoniously surround every square, and where statues stand in silent watch over gardens and parks.

Declared a Unesco World Heritage Site, the city centre has been unmarred by the building boom that has taken over the rest of post-Soviet Russia. But this is no museum-city. St Petersburg is a lively metropolis, packed with clubs, restaurants, theatres and music, with a large population of students and young people, and more traffic and hustle than the city can sometimes manage.

THE NORTHERN CAPITAL

For a young city, St Petersburg has had a surprisingly eventful and turbulent history. Home to the Russian court for over 200 years, its palaces witnessed royal triumphs and sorrows – and not a few assassinations. It was the home of the arts, the city that reinvented ballet, that inspired the best of Russia's poets and writers, and that became home to some of the finest art collections in the world. However, it was also the city that brought down the Romanov dynasty and became the 'cradle of the revolution'. St Petersburg is also the Hero City of Leningrad, which withstood the German army's 900-day blockade during World War II, which Russians call the 'Great Patriotic War'.

In the Soviet period, St Petersburg suffered the rather benign neglect of its leaders. By the end of the Soviet era and in the first years of the new Russian Federation, St Petersburg became a rather run-down, dirty and dowdy city. Even the gilding had faded on the cupolas and spires.

But under the energetic rule of (former) Governor Valentina Matviyenko, the city began reclaiming its birthright. The 300th anni-

Strolling down Nevsky prospekt

versary of the city in 2003 and G8 meetings in 2006 saw an influx of funding that started to transform the city. In addition, while some of the post-Soviet shabbiness remains, most would agree that the city centre has since been greatly improved.

21ST-CENTURY CITY

St Petersburg is one of the world's greatest cities for art-lovers. It is filled with the glories of pre-revolutionary architecture and has the best art collections in Russia; the Hermitage is one of the largest and most dazzling museums anywhere. St Petersburg rivals Moscow in its performing arts, particularly the Kirov ballet, which has preserved and developed the finest traditions of Russian dance. If you tire of urban beauty, you can go out to the 'necklace' of palace estates that encircle the city: the grand blue-and-gold Catherine Palace at Tsarskoe Selo; the more intimate palace of Pavlovsk, nestled in a beautifully landscaped park; or Peterhof,

St Petersburg's waterways have earned it comparisons to Venice

the Russian Versailles, with a breathtaking Grand Palace and parks dotted with hundreds of fountains.

St Petersburg has become quite tourist-friendly, with more signs in English, shops catering to tourists and a good range of hotels and 'mini-hotels'. Thousands of restaurants and cafés offer every kind of cuisine, including wonderfully updated and innovative Russian classics. Things are lively at the city's clubs and bars nearly every night, and visitors can enjoy everything from folk concerts to jazz to reggae.

St Petersburg seems rather small, but this is deceptive: over 5 million people live within the city limits, most of them in housing estates far from the city centre, but connected by public transport. It is a fairly homogeneous population – the vast majority of the residents are Slavs, with smaller populations from the former Soviet republics. People tend to be well dressed in the European manner, and a touch of aristocratic gentility has remained in the city's native residents.

WHEN TO GO

St Petersburg is only six degrees south of the Arctic Circle. Although the sea mitigates the climate, which averages about 20°C (68°F) in the summer and -5°C (23°F) in the winter, the damp can be piercing, and the wind off the Gulf of Finland is wicked. Since it is so far north, the city enjoys the magnificent White Nights in high summer. From mid-June to mid-July, the sky barely darkens, and the city is filled with revellers 24 hours a day. Nevertheless, in the winter, residents and visitors pay for the glorious summer sun with only a few hours of pallid sunlight a day.

The best time to visit is during the summer, when the city never sleeps and all the city's palaces, parks and fountains are open to the public – and when there are arts festivals virtually every week. However, it is also beautiful in deep winter – when snow lies on the gold spires and cupolas the city seems nestled in a white down, and the ice on the rivers and canals glimmers in the weak sun. 'Golden autumn' is a great time for performing-arts lovers who want to enjoy the season's premieres.

Late spring is also good for a visit – before the tourist crowds (and price rises), but with mild weather and the arts in full swing. Only the early spring fails to show the city off at its best, particularly April, when the parks and gardens are closed to dry after the winter. Even then, the celebration of Maslenitsa (Pancake Week) before Lent brings a festive air to the city.

IN TRANSITION

Petersburgers lament that they have an imperial city with a provincial budget. Although there is a great deal of industrial production, Moscow has received the biggest share of the petro-dollars that have fuelled the country's partial economic revival. This is a city still very much in transition. Buildings on smaller lanes have yet to get a new coat of paint and some of the older museums have a musty odour and old-fashioned exhibits.

But that is also the city's charm: corners of St Petersburg are still untouched by time and let you seamlessly drift into the past, to centuries without cars and lifts and the internet. After a few days in St Petersburg, few fail to fall under the city's spell.

A BRIEF HISTORY

St Petersburg's history is brief – just over three centuries. Yet in that time a magnificent city rose out of the marshland, was nearly destroyed by invading armies, plundered by its own people and then slipped into provincial decline, only to rise once again as a great centre of art, beauty and culture.

RUSSIA BEFORE PETER THE GREAT

The Russian empire grew slowly from the 9th century. The successor state to Kievan Rus, Russia was first a jumble of city-states ruled by Grand Princes. Attacked by the Tatars (called Mongols in the West) in the 13th century and kept under their rule for nearly 250 years, the state developed without real contact with European powers. After vanquishing the 'Tatar-Mongol Yoke', Moscow began to gather many of its neighbouring city-states into its sphere of influence. This new state of Russia was tightly connected with the Russian Orthodox Church, which considered itself the successor to the 'fallen Church' of Rome and Constantinople.

After the original ruling house came to an end, a period of chaos ensued called the 'Time of Troubles'. A new dynasty appeared in 1613, when Mikhail Romanov took the crown. Russia under the first Romanovs had a prosperous and grand capital in Moscow and was more Eastern than Western in appearance, outlook and customs.

Peter's foundations

According to legend, when the foundation was being laid for the Peter and Paul Fortress, an eagle soared in the sky, a sign of divine approbation.

PETER'S CITY

Then came the Romanov who would be called Peter the Great. Traumatised by a rebellion that took the lives of his family, Peter largely grew up on the outskirts of the capital. A giant of a man (2 metres/6ft 7in tall) with enormous energy, curiosity and a keen mind, he set off to Europe incognito to study the crafts, arts, sciences and state institutions of Russia's European

Peter the Great

neighbours. After putting down several rebellions in his home country, he crowned himself emperor and began a series of reforms to inject a little European civilisation into his domain.

In 1700 Peter the Great declared war on Sweden, which at the time controlled the majority of the Baltic Sea region. By 1703 Russia had taken the entire length of the Neva river, and Peter founded a new port, which he called Sankt Pieter Burkh, in the Dutch manner, after his patron saint. Peter envisioned a planned city, with streets laid out in a regular grid and civic architecture designed around squares and gardens. It was to be a rational, Western city – the opposite of Eastern Moscow, with its streets scattered erratically around the Kremlin. The conditions during construction were appalling: it is thought that up to 100,000 workers died of fever and disease in the marshy land. The Russian court baulked at moving to this wilderness, but Peter insisted, and in 1712 he forced 1,000 noble families and 500 merchant families to move north. By the time of Peter's death in 1725 the city's population had risen to 40,000.

THE AGE OF THE EMPRESSES

After Peter's death, his wife Catherine and then grandson Peter rebelled and moved the court back to Moscow. However, Empress Anna (reigned 1730–40) returned the court to St Petersburg, hired Bartolomeo Rastrelli as court architect and began to commission the city's magnificent Russian Baroque palaces. Anna and her successor, the Empress Elizabeth (reigned 1741–62) were great lovers of stately balls and aesthetic beauty. Under Elizabeth, the Winter Palace, Smolny Convent and Catherine Palace were begun, while Peterhof was redesigned.

⊘ ANNA'S ICE PALACE

During the early years of the St Petersburg court, emperors and empresses had 'court jokers' – usually noblemen who had displeased the ruler or defied the law. During the reign of Empress Anna, Prince Mikhail Golitsyn married an Italian woman and converted to Catholicism. The enraged empress annulled the marriage and designated the prince as one of her court jokers. For a laugh, she decided to marry her Kalmyk maid to the prince and built a honeymoon palace for them on the Neva river by the Winter Palace. Over 17 metres (56ft) long and 5 metres (16.5ft) wide, the palace was made of carved blocks of ice, as were its furnishings: furniture, clocks, flowers in vases and even cards laid out on an ice table – all lit by thousands of candles in ice candlesticks. The poor couple somehow survived their wedding night in the palace, which stood on the frozen river during February and March of 1740.

The second Catherine became known as Catherine the Great (1762–96). The German wife of Peter III, she ended her husband's brief rule with a coup and assumed the throne. She was both famously liberal, corresponding with Voltaire and instituting some key reforms, and famously imperious and imperial, squashing a peasant rebellion and enlarging the Russian empire. Her building spree introduced neoclassicism to the capital, and she built the Little and Old Hermitages, the Hermitage Theatre and the Marble Palace, as well as the Bronze Horseman, the statue of Peter the Great. Under the reign of these empresses, St Petersburg ceased to be an oasis of luxury in the wilderness and finally became the grand capital that Peter had envisioned.

STUMBLING TOWARDS REFORM

When Catherine died, her son Paul ruled briefly (1796–1801), before being killed in his bed during a palace coup. His son Alexander came to the throne. The entire 19th century was ruled by tsars named Alexander and Nicholas, who moved towards and away from modern democratic institutions. Each ruler built new palaces and cathedrals, squares and monuments, bringing their own style and vision to Peter's city. By the end of the century, St Petersburg was a vibrant capital, filled with artists, poets, writers, scientists and scholars, as well as a growing population of merchants and industrialists – and a vast population of artisans and working people.

Alexander I (reigned 1801–25) began as a moderate reformer, but became more conservative over the course of his reign. During his reign, Russia was attacked by the French armies under Napoleon's command; they captured the Kremlin before being forced into retreat. The General Staff Building and the Alexander Column, erected in honour of the hard-won victory over Napoleon, completed the architectural ensemble of Palace Square. Alexander I also had the Strelka redesigned, with a new Stock Exchange building and the landmark Rostral Columns.

The reign (1825–55) of his brother, Nicholas I, is remembered for the Decembrist uprising – a group of noblemen and

Alexander II, surrounded by his family

officers who called for a constitution and were exe-cuted or exiled to Siberia for their heresy. Nicholas I had his favourite architect, Carlo Rossi, design the buildings of the Senate and Alexandrinskaya ploshchad (now Ostrovskovo), one of the most aesthetically pleasing squares in the city. Nicholas also had the first railroad built (in 1837, between the city and Tsarskoe Selo) and the first permanent bridge over the Neva.

Alexander II (1855–81) was the 'Tsar Liberator' who freed the serfs and insti-tuted a number of important reforms. However, the eman-cipation of the serfs and nascent industrialisation brought thou-sands of the poor into the city. Tenements went up to house them, and grander apartment buildings appeared for the growing middle class. The arts flourished, but social inequities worsened. This enlightened tsar might have responded to stem the tide of rebel-lion, but was killed by an assassin's bomb before he could do so.

His son, Alexander III (reigned 1881–94) did not rule for long, and his time at the state's helm was reactionary and conservative. When he died suddenly in 1894, his son Nicholas II found himself on the throne; a kind and pious man utterly unprepared for the role history had thrust on him. In 1904 the 'short, victorious war'

Grigory Rasputin

When Nicholas II's son and heir, Alexei, was found to be suffering from haemophilia, the desperate Empress Alexandra turned to Grigory Rasputin, a debauched Si-berian peasant who claimed to be a mystical healer. Somehow he managed to ease the Tsarevich's suffer-ing, and Alexandra fell under his spell. One of the tsar's advisers wrote: "His wife ruled the state and Rasputin ruled her. Rasputin inspired, the empress ordered, the tsar obeyed." Rasputin was eventually killed in 1916 by a group of noblemen.

that he foolishly instigated with Japan ended with the destruction of the Russian navy, then in 1905 he was implicated in the massacre of peaceful demonstrators on 'Bloody Sunday'. All the while, he struggled with his own family tragedy of an ailing heir (see box page 19). He blundered into the new century, doing nothing to stop the unrest and seemingly doing everything to make it worse.

While the empire seemed to slide towards collapse, the city continued to grow, especially with *style moderne* (Art Nouveau) mansions and apartment buildings that blended perfectly with the Baroque and neoclassical legacy.

What's in a name?

In August 1914, with Russia at war with Germany, Nicholas II ordered the city name changed to Petrograd (*grad* is the old Russian word for city). Three days after Vladimir Lenin's death in 1924, the name was changed to Leningrad. In 1991 the residents voted to restore the city's original name, although when the war years are remembered, Leningrad is often used in memory of those who died under that name and the surrounding administrative region is still called Leningradskaya oblast. Among Russians the city is often referred to as simply 'Peter'.

THE REVOLUTION

When Russia entered World War I in 1914, it suffered enormous losses. The poverty-stricken, weary and deprived population had reached the end of its tether. In March 1917, the last tsar, Nicholas II, abdicated and was succeeded by a Provisional Government. Vladimir Lenin, a professional revolutionary, saw his chance to exploit the chaos and discontent. He and his comrades arrived at Finland Station in April 1917 and made brief rousing remarks to a crowd of workers that had been rallied at the station.

Lenin and his Bolsheviks jockeyed for power in the workers' soviets (councils), which countered the Provisional Government. On the night of 25 October 1917 they set in motion a coup d'état. The battleship *Aurora* famously fired a blank shot that signalled the start of the coup. Their soldiers claimed the city's strategic railway stations, post office, banks and bridges, and then finally escorted the Provisional Government out

Russian revolutionaries pile onto a lorry in 1917

of the Winter Palace. Few shots were fired. At first the rest of the country had little idea that anything had happened at all.

The Bolshevik hold on power was not absolute at first, and they moved the capital to Moscow in 1918 to ensure greater safety. The coup turned into a civil war, which lasted until 1922. St Petersburg's first year of Soviet power was marked by bitter poverty, famine and violence, first born of chaos and then used as a tool of state repression. The tsar, his family and relatives were murdered in Yekaterinburg in 1918. Private housing was turned into communal apartments; palaces and mansions were claimed as state offices or turned into museums; churches were dynamited or made into dormitories, warehouses or offices. The population fled; in 1915 the city had over 2 million inhabitants, by 1920 there were fewer than 800,000.

The city of the arts began to lose its geniuses. The artistic elite emigrated, died of hunger, were silenced by the censors, or worse – sent to prison, exile or the executioner. Economically the city began to revive somewhat in the 1930s, when Stalin began his great industrialisation effort and decided to move the centre of the city south, starting work on the enormous House of Soviets that was to be the heart of Leningrad. But economic revival was accompanied by purges of the Party, military and industrial elite in waves of campaigns to rid the country of 'anti-Soviet elements'. While figures are still debated, it is certain that at least 1 million people were killed in the repressions, including top military leaders.

WORLD WAR II

The loss of the army's best leaders was one reason the country was unprepared for Hitler's forces when they attacked on 22 June 1941. The Nazi armies quickly moved through the west of the country and by September had arrived on the outskirts of Leningrad. Most of the treasures in the city's museums were packed and shipped east by train, and whatever could not be removed was buried underground or hidden by netting and camouflage. For 900 days, from 8 September 1941 to 27 January 1944, the Germans blockaded and relentlessly bombed the city.

Secret documents discovered after the war showed the Wehrmacht's intention to destroy the population. One read: 'The Führer is determined to eliminate the city of Petersburg from the face of earth.' Hitler planned to celebrate New Year 1942 in the imperial palaces and even printed invitations to a reception at the Astoria Hotel. During that winter the constant bombing destroyed the already scant food supplies, and rations decreased to 400g/15oz of bread for a worker and 200g/7.5oz for a woman or child. As the winter continued, rations were reduced further still, to 250g/9oz and 125g/4.5oz respectively.

Some relief came with the opening of the Road of Life across the frozen Lake Ladoga, but supplies only resumed when the blockade was broken in 1944. By then much of the city had been destroyed, virtually all of the suburban palaces had been plundered, burned and blown up. Over 1 million people died, but the German divisions never entered the city.

COLLAPSE OF THE SOVIET UNION

The city was rebuilt after the war, but throughout the late Soviet period, it had a rather odd status: a cultural capital equal to Moscow with services at the level of provincial Tula. Perhaps it is no wonder that when Mikhail Gorbachev came to power in 1985 and introduced his policies of *glasnost* (openness) and *perestroika* (restructuring) – designed to help the nation to face up to its

Peterhof was captured and all but destroyed by German troops during World War II

backwardness and revamp its moribund economy – St Petersburg became one of the strongest centres pushing for reform.

When a group of hardliners in the Soviet government organised a coup in August 1991, the leadership and population of the city were determined to defend their rights. The Kirov factory provided fax communications with the centre of resistance led by Boris Yeltsin in Moscow, Mayor Anatoly Sobchak defied the State Emergency Committee (the coup organisers) on local television, taxi drivers used their radios to pass on information about possible troop movements and nearly 200,000 people streamed into Palace Square. No troops entered the city. By the end of three tense days, the city and nation had left their Soviet past behind. At the end of 1991, the Soviet Union was disbanded and the Russian Federation tricolour flag appeared on the city's spires for the first time in over 70 years.

The city, like the country as a whole, suffered greatly in the economic upheavals of the 1990s, as leaders dismantled the old system, while struggling with corruption and an old guard eager to turn back the clock. Hyperinflation, devaluation of the rouble and the default on government loans in 1998 wiped out people's savings. The absence of a modern legal and banking system thwarted new business growth. St Petersburg did not reap immediate economic benefits from post-Soviet economic change; indeed, it got more gangsters than businessmen, and its beautiful palaces and museums became run-down and derelict.

The city finally got its break in 2000, when Vladimir Putin came to power. A native of the city, Putin began to shower it with funds. Increased foreign and domestic investment and plans to move the Constitutional Court to the city's former Senate buildings have been helping St Petersburg repair a century of damage and bring new life, business and art to the northern capital.

HISTORICAL LANDMARKS

1703 Peter the Great founds the city.

1712 The imperial court is moved to the city.

1725 Catherine I moves the capital back to Moscow after Peter's death.

1730 Empress Anna returns the capital to St Petersburg.

1754 Rastrelli begins the Winter Palace.

1762 Catherine II (the Great) begins her reign.

1801 Catherine II's son Paul is murdered; Alexander I takes the throne.

1812 Napoleon's armies attack Russia and capture the Kremlin.

1825 The Decembrist rebellion.

1851 The rail line opens between Moscow and St Petersburg.

1855 Alexander II assumes the throne.

1858 St Isaac's Cathedral is completed after 40 years.

1861 The emancipation of the serfs.

1881 Alexander II is assassinated and Alexander III assumes the throne.

1894 Nicholas II assumes the throne.

1904–5 Russo-Japanese War.

1913 300th anniversary of the Romanov dynasty.

1914 Russia enters World War I and the city is renamed Petrograd.

1917 In February the tsar abdicates; in October the Bolsheviks stage a coup against the Provisional Government.

1918 Capital moved to Moscow; imperial family killed in Yekaterinburg.

1922 Civil war ends with the formation of the USSR.

1924 Lenin dies and the city is renamed Leningrad.

1941–4 900-day blockade of Leningrad during World War II.

1991 The USSR is dissolved and the city is renamed St Petersburg.

1999 Boris Yeltsin, first president of Russia, resigns on 31 December.

2000 Vladimir Putin, son of St Petersburg, elected president.

2008 Zenit St Petersburg football team wins the UEFA Cup.

2017 A terrorist bomb explodes on St Petersburg metro, killing 15 and injuring 45 people.

2018 Presidential election scheduled for March. In June and July, Russia, including St Petersburg, is set to host the FIFA World Cup.

The splendid Winter Palace

WHERE TO GO

Although St Petersburg is a sprawling metropolis with a population of over 5 million, the historical centre is fairly compact. The city is bisected by the Neva river, which splits into the Bolshaya (Great) and Malaya (Small) Neva at its widest point near the Spit and Hare Island. Although canals and rivers snake through the city, the streets are laid out in a grid, with the central thoroughfare of Nevsky prospekt cutting through the city, and squares and parks at major intersections. For the purposes of this guide, we have divided the city into six geographically distinct sections. A final section describes some of the palaces in the 'necklace' of suburban estates that rings the city.

St Petersburg's grid plan and well-marked streets make it easy to navigate on foot. To get from one end of Nevsky prospekt to the other, you can jump on one of the buses or trolleybuses that ply the main street, and to get across town, it's easy to hop on the efficient metro. For a trip out of the city, there are tour buses every day, or freelance guides with drivers. In the summer months, the most enjoyable way to get to Peterhof is by hydrofoil along the Neva.

St Petersburg's huge art and historical museums can seem daunting to visitors with just a few days in the city. The Hermitage likes to tell visitors that it would take 15 years of daily eight-hour visits to spend just a minute on each of the treasures in its vast collection – and that

Bridges

One of the most charming sights of St Petersburg is the opening of the bridges over the Neva – unless you are on the wrong side of the river. The bridges open from about 12.30am to 6am from April to November.

is just one museum in this museum-laden city. Unless money is a concern, the best way to see the Hermitage and other museums is in small increments each day, with breaks for shopping, a bite to eat, and the other pleasures of the city.

PETROGRAD SIDE

The Petrograd Side (Петроградская сторона – Petrogradskaya storona) encompasses three main islands, including **Hare Island** (Заячий остров – Zayachy ostrov), the small island where the city began, **Petrograd Island** (Петроградский остров – Petgrogradsky ostrov) and **Aptekarsky Island** (Аптекарский остров). Peter laid the foundations for the Peter and Paul Fortress here, and the islands were largely populated by workers, artisans and merchants, until the Trinity Bridge over the Neva was completed in 1903. The building boom on the Petrograd Side coincided with the passion for *style moderne* (Art Nouveau) architecture, and the island is considered to have the best and most numerous examples of this style in the city, especially along Kamennoostrovsky prospekt. Most of the sights are a comfortable walk from the city's beginnings in the Peter and Paul Fortress on the banks of the Neva.

PETER AND PAUL FORTRESS

Peter and Paul Fortress ❶ (Петропавловская крепость – Petropavlovskaya krepost; www.spbmuseum.ru; Tue 11am–6pm, Thu–Mon 11am–7pm), where the city began, was originally built of wood and called Sankt Pieter Burkh in honour of the Apostle St Peter. Although it was built to withstand an attack from the Swedes, its battlements were never tested. Over the centuries its structures have served as a prison, a mint, the resting place of the imperial family and the first rocket-engine laboratory (in the 1930s). Today it is part of the Museum of St Petersburg's History (see page 64), and despite its rather dark past, it is a fascinating place, with one of Russia's most beautiful cathedrals and a number of museums that give an excellent introduction to the history of the city.

Peter and Paul Cathedral

The stone walls of the fortress, built in 1706–40 by Domenico Trezzini, have six bastions named after Peter the Great's closest companions: the Gosuradev (the sovereign), Menshikov, Golovkin, Zotov, Trubetskoy and Naryshkin. The main entrance, at the northwest corner, is through two gates: the rather plain **Ivan's Gate** (Иоанновские ворота – Ioannovskie vorota), built in 1730, and the lavish **Peter's Gate** (Петровские ворота – Petrovskie vorota), built in 1717–18 by Trezzini. Above the Peter's Gate portal is the two-headed eagle and a bas-relief carved by Conradt Osner for the first wooden gate. It depicts the Apostle Peter casting down Simon Magus – a symbol of Peter's victory over the Swedes. On either side of the portal are niches with statues of Bellona, the Roman goddess of war, and Minerva, the goddess of wisdom and crafts.

The main gate to the river, the **Neva Gate** (Невские ворота – Nevskie vorota), was built in 1730–1 and redesigned to its present austere classical appearance in 1787. To the west of

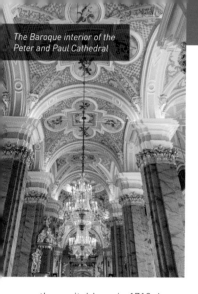

the gate is a narrow strip of land between the fortress and water, which is covered with sunbathers in good weather. In the winter, human 'walruses' break the ice for a quick dip in the frigid water.

PETER AND PAUL CATHEDRAL

The fortress originally had a small wooden chapel dedicated to Sts Peter and Paul, but when Peter the Great moved the capital here in 1712, he commissioned Trezzini to build the **Peter and Paul Cathedral ❷** (Петропавловский собор – Petropavlovsky sobor; Mon–Fri 10am–7pm, slightly shorter hours Sat–Sun), which would be Russia's main house of worship. Legend has it that Peter took part in the design himself, insisting on the architectural innovation of an enormous spire covered in gold. The height of the cathedral is 122.5 metres (402ft), of which 30 metres (98ft) is the spire itself. Originally made of gilded wood, after several fires it was finally changed to steel in 1857–8.

The interior of the cathedral was also an innovation. Instead of the traditional Russian Orthodox cross plan, it is built in the style of Western churches; a long rectangle divided into three naves by enormous pilasters. It is a magnificent example of early Baroque architecture; pale-green and rose pilasters, glittering chandeliers and a many-tiered carved and gilded wooden iconostasis reminiscent of a triumphal arch with 43 icons. The cathedral is the resting place of all the tsars after Peter the Great, with the exception of Peter II, who is interred in the Kremlin. In 1998, after lengthy forensic investigations, remains unearthed outside of Yekaterinburg were determined to be the imperial family, and Nicholas II, Alexandra and three daughters were laid to rest here.

Next to the cathedral is the **Mausoleum of the Grand Dukes** (Великокняжеская усыпальница – Velikoknyazheskaya usypalnitsa), built in 1896–1906 by the architect David Grimm, where 60 members of the imperial family are buried. Nearby is the **Boat House** (Ботный дом – Botny dom), where Peter the Great's first boat was originally displayed (now found in the Central Navy Museum; see page 37).

The fortress was used as a prison even as it was being built. Peter the Great incarcerated his son Alexei, whom he accused of treason, in the 'Secret House' here in 1718, where he was tortured to death (possibly with the tsar's participation). Before the house was demolished, the Decembrists (see page 18) were also held here before execution, as was writer Fyodor Dostoevsky. In 1872 the **Trubetskoy Bastion** was turned into a prison, where an illustrious group of political prisoners were held, including the ministers of the tsar and members of the imperial family and Provisional Government. It was turned into a museum in 1924. Visitors can see cells,

Laying Peter to rest

Peter the Great did not live to see his cathedral completed; he died in 1725 and was interred in a wooden chapel inside the cathedral. When the cathedral was completed in 1733 and consecrated, he was placed in the church's first crypt.

punishment rooms and the guardroom, as well as an exhibition of photographs and other artefacts from the history of the prison.

The two-floored **Commandant's House** (1743–6) and the **Engineer's House** (1748–9) display temporary and permanent exhibitions about the history of the city.

KRONVERK AND THE EMBANKMENT

Fearing attacks from the fortress's vulnerable landward side to the north, Peter the Great had a series of earthen battlements, ditches, a moat and weaponry installed in what is called **Kronverk** (Кронверк), because the shape of the area looked like a crown. In the 19th century it was the site of the execution of the Decembrists, and was then used to house the arsenal. Pyotr Tamansky designed the horseshoe-shaped brick building in 1849–60. Today it is the **Military-Historical Museum** (Военно-исторический музей артиллерии – Voenno-istorichesky muzey artillerii; Alexandrovsky Park 7; www.artillery-museum.ru; Wed–Sun 11am–6pm), which displays every kind of weapon used in Russia, along with tanks, banners, flags, uniforms and other military equipment.

Behind the Artillery Museum is the **Alexandrovsky Park**, a stretch of land that was originally left empty so that enemies could be easily spied creeping up on the

Shemyakin's statue

Near the cathedral is the avant-garde artist Mikhail Shemyakin's statue of Peter the Great, placed in 1991. The odd sculpture, with its disproportioned head and hands, scandalised city residents when it was installed. It now seems to have been accepted: people can be seen rubbing Peter's right index finger for good luck.

fortress. In the mid-19th century it was turned into a park, and until the revolution offered a combination of genteel and rowdy pleasures, from an opera house to the zoo. Today it has cafés, casinos, a zoo (see page 96), an amusement park and a planetarium (daily 10.30am–6pm).

Near the entrance to the Peter and Paul Fortress is **Trinity Square**, once the site of a cathedral and the first Stock

Stained-glass windows at the Museum of Political History

Exchange, and the bustling centre of life on the island. Nearby is the **Museum of Political History** ❸ (Музей политической истории – Muzey politicheskoy istorii; ulitsa Kuybisheva 2/4; www.polithistory.ru; Sat–Tue 10am–6pm, Wed and Fri until 8pm), housed in two now-united *style moderne* mansions owned by the ballerina Matilda Kshesynskaya and Baron Brandt. Kshesynskaya's house was commandeered by Lenin and his cohorts in 1917 and now displays Lenin's preserved study, photographs, posters and other political memorabilia, and includes constantly running videos from virtually every era, as well as tapes of the leaders' speeches. Several rooms recreate life in the Kshesynskaya mansion when the prima ballerina lived there.

On the bank of the Neva stands the little house that Peter the Great first lived in when he began to build his city. The log **Cabin of Peter the Great** ❹ (Домик Петра – Domik Petra I;

The imposing Cruiser Aurora

Petrovskaya nab. 6; http://en.rusmuseum.ru; Fri–Mon and Wed 10am–6pm, Thu 1–9pm) was built 24–26 May 1703 and is the only wooden structure from the Petrine period to survive to this day. In 1844, a brick shell was built around it to protect it from St Petersburg's destructive climate. Inside are the rustic little rooms where this giant of a tsar lived until 1708, whenever he was in the city.

A bit further down on the embankment is the famous **Cruiser** *Aurora* ❺ (Крейсер Аврора – Kreyser Avrora, Petrovskaya nab; www.aurora.org.ru; Wed–Sun 11am–6pm) that fired the blank shot to signal the attack on the Winter Palace in 1917. The ship was built in 1900 and served in the ill-fated Russo-Japanese War before being turned into a training vessel. Today the ship's crew quarters, machinery and famous weaponry are all open to visitors, along with lots of revolutionary memorabilia.

If you want to know what life was like in the early Soviet period, visit the apartment where Sergey Kirov, the head of the city's Party administration lived in 1926–34. The **Kirov Museum ❻** (Музей С.М. Кирова – Muzey S.M. Kirova; Kamennoostrovsky prospekt 26/28; http://kirovmuseum.ru; Thu–Tue 11am–6pm) is a bit like walking back in time, since everything – bedroom slippers, books, hunting trophies, art – is intact, as is his office, taken from the Party headquarters. There are exhibits of photographs and memorabilia from his life and mysterious death, as well as a fascinating and detailed exhibition on childhood during the Stalinist era that recreates settings from children's life in the 1920s and 1930s.

KIROV ISLANDS

The **Kirov Islands** (Киров-ские острова – Kirovskie ostrova), to the northeast of Petrograd Side, are three pretty havens from urban life. **Kamenny** is rapidly becoming a gated community for the rich and famous; **Krestovsky** is dominated by the large Victory Park; **Yelagin** is home to a lovely park and **Yelagin Palace** (Wed–Sun 10am–6pm), a neoclassical mansion built in 1818–22 by Carlo Rossi for Alexander I's mother. The primary joy of all three

Sergey Kirov

Sergey Kirov (1886–1934) was a leading revolutionary who headed St Petersburg's Party organisation and city administration from 1926 until his death. A good manager, charismatic speaker and popular leader, he was a close friend of Joseph Stalin. In 1934 he was shot in the back of the head as he entered his office in the Smolny Institute. Historians believe that Stalin ordered his death as a pretext for launching his Great Purges.

islands is nature; paths winding through woods and along riverbanks are filled with families and friends enjoying a break from the city.

VASILEVSKY ISLAND

Peter the Great originally planned for Vasilevsky Island (Васильевский остров – Vasilevsky ostrov) to be the administrative centre of his new city, with canals cut in straight lines across the island. He built several administrative buildings, but flooding and lack of access from the southern side of the river (and the road to Moscow) put an end to his plans. Many of his administration buildings are now educational institutions or museums, and the intended canals are city streets with the unusual name of 'lines'. Most of the attractions are near the Strelka (Spit), but Bolshoy prospekt and the quiet, largely residential 'lines' are pleasant for strolls.

STRELKA

The Spit (Стрелка – Strelka) is a triangle of land that juts out where the Neva divides into the Bolshaya and Malaya Neva rivers. The architecture here was designed by Thomas de Thomon and Andreyan Zakharov in 1810: the monumental Stock Exchange flanked by two warehouses overlooking a small park with two mighty lighthouses. The lighthouses, called the **Rostral Columns** (Ростральные колонны – Rostralnye kolonny, from the Latin *rostra*, a stage in Rome decorated with the prows of captured ships), are 32 metres (105ft) high and decorated with allegorical images of Russia's four great rivers: the Neva, Volga, Dnieper and Volkhov. They were originally lit with oil lamps as navigational lights.

Vasilevsky Island

The classical Stock Exchange is now the **Central Naval Museum** (Центральный Военно-морской музей – Tsentralny Voenno-morskoy muzey; Birzhevaya ploshchad 4; www.naval museum.ru; Wed–Sun 11am–6pm), crammed full of every kind of ship and nautical device, including Peter the Great's original 'little boat' that he learned to sail in, and a particularly rich collection of Soviet posters, flags and naval and political memorabilia.

The north warehouse that edges the Stock Exchange now houses two institutes; next to it is the former Customs House, now the Institute of Russian Literature. The south warehouse is home to the **Zoological Museum** (Зоологический музей – Zoologichesky muzey; Universitetskaya nab. 1/3; www.zin.ru; Wed–Mon 11am–6pm), with its thousands of pieces of taxidermy from land, air and sea, including some baby mammoths dating back over 40,000 years.

UNIVERSITY EMBANKMENT

Next to the Zoological Museum on the embankment is the **Museum of Anthropology and Ethnography, Kunstkamera ❼** (Музей антропологии и этнографии, Кунст камера – Muzey antropologii i etnografii, Kunstkamera; Universitetskaya nab. 3; www.kunstkamera.ru; Tue–Sun 11am–6pm), a marvellous Petrine Baroque structure built 1718–34 by Georg Johann Mattarnovy to house Peter the Great's Cabinet of Curiosities. Peter I bought them from the Dutch scientist Frederik Ruysch in 1717, and put them on display to dispel his people's superstitions. He wanted them to see that physical abnormalities were natural phenomena and not the work of witches or the devil. The collection of anatomical oddities is displayed in the rotunda to packed crowds of adults and children, although some visitors may find the collection disturbing.

Peter's pal

Alexander Menshikov (1673–1729) was Peter the Great's best friend and companion. Of lowly background, Menshikov had the intelligence and military and administrative skill to win the tsar's favour, and apparently enough charm for the tsar to forgive his greed, embezzling and corrupt practices. After Peter's death, he was stripped of his titles and wealth, and banished to Siberia, where he died.

The museum also has an extensive and truly wonderful collection of apparel and ethnographic artefacts from all over the world. In the circular hall of the tower is the study where Mikhail Lomonosov, Russia's first and most prominent scientist and scholar, worked in 1741–65, and the spectacular **Great Gottorp Globe**, which requires a separate ticket to see. The current globe replaced the original presented to Peter the Great in 1713, which was

The Twelve Colleges

destroyed by fire. Over 3 metres (9ft) in diameter, it shows the world on the outside and the heavens on the inside.

Further west along the embankment of the Bolshaya Neva is the spectacular red-and-white Petrine Baroque building of the **Twelve Colleges** (Двенадцать коллегий – Dvenadtsat kollegy), built in 1743 by Domenico Trezzini and stretching over 400 metres (1,300ft) perpendicular to the river bank. Originally meant for Peter the Great's 'collegium' of ministers, it became part of the university in the 19th century. The entire embankment and neighbourhood is the heart of St Petersburg's academic world, with students and professors dodging tourists on their way to classes.

Nearby is the **Menshikov Palace 8** (Дворец Меншикова – Dvorets Menshikova; Universitetskaya nab. 15; www.hermitagemuseum.org; Tue, Thu, Sat, Sun 10.30am–6pm, Wed and Fri until 9pm; free first Thu of the month), the first stone building in the city, built in 1710–27 by a number of architects

Egyptian sphinxes

On the embankment in front of the Academy of Arts are 14th-century BC sphinxes brought to St Petersburg in 1832.

including Domenico Trezzini, Bartolomeo Rastrelli and Jean-Baptiste Le Blond. Built for Peter the Great's best friend and companion, Prince Alexander Menshikov, whom the sovereign appointed first governor of St Petersburg, the palace served as the official site for foreign receptions and unofficial carousing by Peter and his friends. Restored to its original appearance in 2002, it is a magnificent Petrine Dutch-inspired residence, with halls on a human scale, from the kitchens to the reception rooms decorated with tapestries and silk wallpaper, to the private quarters entirely tiled from floor to ceiling.

Further west is the **Academy of Arts** (Академия Художеств – Akademiya khudozhestv; Universitetskaya nab. 17; http://en.rah.ru; Tue–Sun 11am–6pm), founded in 1757 by the Empress Elizabeth and built by Alexander Kokorinov and Vallin de la Mothe. The imposing neoclassical building has a rather dusty, old-fashioned ambience, with earnest students practising their drawing in the halls of the museum. Most of the Academy's best works were distributed to other museums after the 1917 revolution, but the collection of academic paintings and drawings is worth a look. Be sure to climb up to the top floor to see the architectural scale models of some of the city's most famous structures, including several versions of the Smolny Convent and St Isaac's Cathedral.

THE PALACE EMBANKMENT

It is a rare visitor to St Petersburg who doesn't gasp in awe at the first glimpse of the enormous Palace Square and Winter

Palace. This is the heart and soul of the city, with one of the world's greatest art museums, the Hermitage.

There were three small palaces on this side of the river before Empress Anna commissioned Bartolomeo Rastrelli to build a proper Winter Palace (Зимний дворец – Zimny dvorets) in 1754. Empress Elizabeth wasn't entirely satisfied with Anna's palace and had Rastrelli redo the residence. What you see now was completed in 1762, although parts were reconstructed after a devastating fire in 1837 or slightly modified over the years. The pale minty-blue walls, gold decoration and syncopated columns give the enormous, 1,057-room winter residence of the tsars a lightness that belies its massive size.

Catherine the Great had most of the interiors redecorated in her favourite neoclassical style, but she didn't alter the exteriors and some of Rastrelli's most magnificent halls. She did make one enormous change: although her predecessors had collected art, Catherine was a fanatic, and she built the Little Hermitage and Large Hermitage to hold her growing collection, and then built the theatre to enjoy other artistic pleasures. Nicholas I, another serious collector, commissioned the New Hermitage and in 1852 opened part of the collection to the public as the Imperial Museum,

Hermitage interior

Foreign collections

Russian emperors and empresses filled their collection by purchasing large foreign collections, including those once owned by Robert Walpole, John Lyde-Brown, the Empress Josephine, Cristoforo Barbarigo and Gian Pietro Campana.

with an entryway guarded by 10 magnificent 5-metre (16ft) Atlases (male figures decoratively supporting a building). Today, the entire complex of imperial residence and art museum is housed in these five interconnected buildings on the embankment.

In 1917, after the abdication of the tsar, the Provisional Government took up residence in the Winter Palace. On 25 October 1917, Bolsheviks attacked the palace, although it was not 'stormed' by thousands of workers, as Soviet art and cinema have portrayed it. A few shells were lobbed, some shots were fired, one window was broken and the leaders of the government were escorted to the prison across the river.

PALACE SQUARE

Palace Square ❾ (Дворцовая площадь – Dvortsovaya ploshchad) has always been a place for gatherings, both ceremonial and oppositional. Here the tsars greeted troops and celebrated civic and religious holidays, and here on 'Bloody Sunday' (9 January 1905), a group of peaceful workers led by a priest came to the square with a petition for the tsar (not in residence at the time) and were fired on by troops, igniting the first 1905 revolution. Here Leningraders celebrated the end of the war, and here thousands rallied to express their solidarity with Boris Yeltsin in 1991. Today it is where New Year's and other holidays are celebrated, where rock concerts are held – and where teenagers practise their skateboarding techniques.

In the centre of the square is the extraordinary **Alexander Column**, all 600 tonnes rising up 47.5 metres (156ft) and held aloft by gravity alone. Topped with a bronze angel, the column was designed by Auguste de Montferrand in 1834 in commemoration of the 1812 victory over Napoleon.

The **General Staff Headquarters** ❿ was built in 1819–29 by Carlo Rossi for Nicholas I. A magnificent curving building stretching 580 metres (1,903ft), it seems to embrace and complete the vast open space. The building is cut with a gigantic arch topped with Victory in her chariot. The **General Staff Headquarters Museum** (Музей Генерального штаба – Muzey Generalnovo shtaba; Dvortsovaya ploshchad 6; www.hermitage museum.org; Tue, Thu, Sat, Sun 10.30am–6pm, Wed and Fri until 9pm; free first Thu of the month) is spread over several

The gigantic arch of the General Staff Headquarters

Three million items

The total holdings over the museum are over 3 million items. Only 5–10 percent of the Hermitage collection is on display in the halls.

floors of the building, which was renovated and remodelled inside between 2008 and 2014. The second floor houses the amazing collection of gifts received by Russian tsars over the centuries and the three Art Nouveau rooms; the third floor includes Carl Fabergé memorial rooms, 18th- and 19th-century French art rooms and paintings by Wassily Kandinsky and Kazimir Malevich, including his *Black Square*. On the fourth floor, the museum boasts an impressing collection of 19th- and 20th-century French paintings, including dozens of works by Monet, Renoir, Degas, Pissarro, Van Gogh, Matisse (including *La Danse*, painted 1909–10) and Picasso.

THE WINTER PALACE AND HERMITAGE

The **Winter Palace and Hermitage** ⓫ (Dvortsovaya ploshchad. 2; www.hermitagemuseum.org; Tue, Thu, Sat, Sun 10.30am–6pm, Wed and Fri until 9pm; tours and audio-guide in English; times for separate tours of the two treasure galleries held daily are marked on boards in the vestibule; free first Thu of the month) were turned into a museum in 1917. When the German armies invaded the USSR in 1941, about two-thirds of the collection was transported to the Urals; the rest was moved to the lower floors. Despite over 30 bomb attacks and devastating destruction due to water, snow and ice, the palaces survived the war.

Over the decades, the museum collection changed – some works were moved to other Soviet museums or sold, others were expropriated from vast private collections or received as 'trophy art' from Germany and Europe during World War II.

Pieces belonging to this last group of artworks are still highly contested, but for now they remain in St Petersburg.

As the palace buildings are set around courtyards, to many the museum is a confused (and badly signposted) labyrinth. The collection is organised by country and era; the plan available at the information desk makes navigation easier, though not entirely simple.

First (ground) floor

The ground floor displays the museum's excellent collections of works from antiquity, including some spectacular Roman statuary and mosaics, as well as fine and applied art from ancient Egypt, the Caucasus and the ancient East. You will also find art objects from Dagestan, Georgia and Armenia, as well as 15–19th-century Middle Eastern weaponry.

Second floor

On the second floor of the Winter Palace are staterooms, private quarters, ballrooms and other living areas of the imperial families. The living quarters on the far west side include the rooms that the last Romanov children lived in, a wonderful **Oak Library** and the **Small Dining Room** where the Bolsheviks arrested the Provisional Government. The **Dark Corridor** is lined

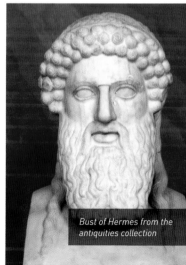

Bust of Hermes from the antiquities collection

The magnificent Jordan Staircase

with tapestries and was once lit by holes in the floor of the third-floor corridor above it, which was itself illuminated by lanterns on the roof. Beyond are the **Golden Drawing Room** and a number of sumptuous boudoirs and sleeping chambers. The staterooms are largely on the Neva side of the palace. In the **Great Hall** (or Nicholas Hall), the largest room in the palace, 5,000 guests could gather and dance. The **Peter the Great Hall** (also called the Small Throne Room), which now displays temporary exhibitions, has an English silver-gilt throne made in 1731.

Perhaps the most spectacular space in the Winter Palace is not a room, but a staircase; the great **Jordan Staircase** built by Rastrelli in 1762. Gracefully proportioned and lavishly decorated in the Baroque style, it was originally called the Ambassadorial Staircase, since ambassadors used it to ascend to see the tsar. It became the Jordan Staircase as it was used by the imperial family to descend to the Neva on Epiphany (celebrated before the revolution on 6 January), the church holiday that celebrates Christ's christening in the Jordan river. On this holiday a hole would be cut in the Neva, from which water would be drawn in a special cup, blessed by the Metropolitan – St Petersburg's religious leader – and drunk by the tsar.

The second floors of the buildings display the majority of the museum's vast art collection; French art of the 15th–18th centuries (including works by Poussin, Lorrain and Fragonard); Spanish art (including several canvases by El Greco, the pride of which is *The Apostles Peter and Paul*); the British collection (a particularly large collection of portraits); the German, Dutch and Flemish collections, which include 40 works by Rubens, canvases by van Dyck and an enormous number of paintings by Rembrandt; and the famed collection of Italian art. In the latter you can find works by Titian, Michelangelo, two canvases by Leonardo da Vinci, including his *Madonna Benois*, and works by Raphael. Other rooms contain extensive collections of medieval European art and armour.

On the second floor of the **Little Hermitage** is the **Pavilion Hall**, an enormous gilded room that overlooks the Hanging Gardens planted by Catherine the Great. The room, lit by nearly 30 chandeliers, has Roman and Byzantine mosaics on the floor and the spectacular **Peacock Clock** made by James Fox in 1772. On the hour, the peacock spreads its wings, and a rooster, owl and mushrooms begin to move. When working, it is demonstrated every Wednesday at 5pm.

Third floor

The third floor displays the collection of 4–12th-century Byzantine art and 18th- and 19th-century Japanese and Chinese art. On view are also Persian miniatures and drawings, as well as Tibetan, Indian and Mongolian art objects. Several rooms are also devoted to the Islamic art of the Middle East.

Henri Matisse's Red Room

EAST TOWARDS THE SUMMER GARDENS

The area east of Palace Square is filled with people, shops and arcades, museums, palaces and some of the city's most famous and lovely squares and gardens. This section covers the sight-filled area around the Moika river bounded by the Fontanka in the east and stretching to the Neva river in the north.

Near Palace Square on the Moika river is the **Apartment Museum of Alexander Pushkin** ⑫ (Музей-квартира А.С. Пушкина – Muzey-kvartira A.S. Pushkina; Wed–Mon 10.30am–6pm, closed last Fri of the month; www.museumpushkin.ru), where Russia's premier poet lived and then died in 1837, after fighting a duel to defend his wife's honour. The apartment has been reconstructed on the basis of sketches and is filled with Pushkin's possessions.

The street that starts on Palace Square and runs east is called **Millionaire's Street** (Миллионная улица – Millionannaya ulitsa),

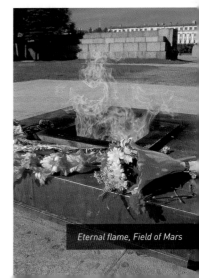

named for the lavish mansions owned by the aristocracy. Today it is a bit down at heel, but at the east end stands the impressive **Marble Palace** (Мраморный дворец – Mramorny dvorets; Millionnaya ulitsa 5; http://en.rusmuseum.ru; Fri–Mon and Wed 10am–6pm, Thu 1pm–9pm), built by Rinaldi in 1768–85 for Catherine the Great's lover Grigory Orlov. A fine example of early classicism, it is ornamented with over 30 kinds and colours of marble, most spectacularly in the **Grand Staircase**, where the soft hues of marble glow under the crystal chandelier. Today it is part of the Russian Museum, exhibiting a private collection of applied and fine arts from the 18th and 19th centuries and an odd assortment of Russian contemporary art, as well as a collection donated by Peter and Irene Ludwig.

To the south of the Marble Palace is the **Field of Mars** (Марсово Поле – Marsovo Pole), used for military parades and festivities starting in 1805. The Soviets appropriated it as a burial ground for the victims of the 1905 revolution; they added a monument to the **Heroes of the Revolution** in 1919 and then an eternal flame in 1957.

On the east side of the narrow Lebyazhnaya Canal are the **Summer Gardens** ⓭ (Летный сад – Letny sad; http://en.rus museum.ru; Wed–Mon May–Sept 10am–10pm, Oct–Mar until 8pm), where

Eternal flame, Field of Mars

Peter the Great built his summer home in a corner of a formal garden with 250 statues and fountains cleverly fed by the river. Although his home survived the disastrous flood of 1777, virtually everything else was destroyed. It was redesigned under Catherine the Great with 92 statues in a natural setting. Throughout the pre-revolutionary period, it was the favourite place for well-born Petersburgers to stroll, chat, flirt and enjoy music and nature. So revered was this garden that not a single tree was felled for firewood during the WWII siege of the city.

In the northeast corner stands Peter's **Summer Palace** ⑭ (Летный дворец – Letny dvorets; http://en.rusmuseum. ru; closed for restoration at the time of writing), a marvellous Dutch-style two-storey home built in 1711 by Trezzini. It is filled with carefully preserved artefacts from Peter's life, including a four-poster bed and the cabinets that once held his Cabinet of Curiosities.

The charming neo-classical **Tea and Coffee Houses** are now used to show temporary art and other exhibits.

SALT TOWN

To the east of the Fontanka is an area that was once called Salt Town (Соляной городок – Solyanoy gorodok), where the state used to store its supplies of salt and wine. Today it is a lovely neighbourhood

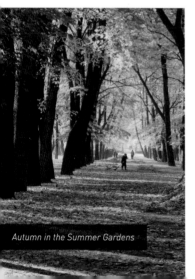

Autumn in the Summer Gardens

of tree-shaded streets notable for two museums. The **Stieglitz Museum** ⓫, also called the **Museum of Applied Art** (Музей прикладного искусства – Muzey prikladnovo iskusstva; Solyanoy pereulok 13–15; www.stieglitzmuseum. ru; Tue–Sat 11am–5pm) is part of an industrial design

school, founded in 1876 by Baron Alexander Stieglitz. To educate his students, he purchased over 30,000 examples of the finest European and Russian applied arts and commissioned a building from Maximilian Messmacher to display them.

After the 1917 revolution, Stieglitz's collection and school were expropriated, and the palatial halls that imitated rooms in Italian Renaissance, Flemish, Baroque and medieval Muscovite style were partitioned or plastered over. Right now it is a jumble of magnificence: glittering halls decorated with tiles, painting and gilding packed willy-nilly with precious European and Russian furniture, ceramics and other applied art from the 16th to 20th centuries.

Next to this museum is the **Museum of the Defence and Blockade of Leningrad** (Музей обороны и блокады Ленинграда – Muzey oborony i blokady Leningrada; Solyanoy pereulok 9; Thu–Mon 10am–6pm, Wed 12.30–8.30pm), opened within months of the lifting of the siege to preserve the memory of those tragic and heroic 900 days. Although there is little in English, most of the extensive exhibitions showing daily life during the blockade and the military operations to take and defend the city are wordlessly eloquent.

NEVSKY PROSPEKT AND AROUND

Nevsky prospekt stretches across the city for 4.5km (3 miles) from the Palace Square to the Alexander Nevsky Lavra. It is the city's chief artery, filled with people day and night, with shops, cafés, arcades, restaurants and many of the city's main attractions along and off the thundering thoroughfare. This section describes the sights of Nevsky prospekt from Palace Square in the west to Ploshchad Vostaniya in the east, including a diversion north to Arts Square to take in the excellent Russian Museum and the remarkable Church 'On Spilled Blood'.

At Palace Square, Nevsky prospekt is a rather dark corridor shadowed by tall buildings. On School No. 210 on the north of the street is a sign preserved from World War II: "Citizens! This side of the street is more dangerous during a bomb attack!" At the corner of the Politseysky Bridge is the **Literary Café**, formerly Wolf and Beranger's, where Pushkin stopped on his way to his fatal duel. On the south corner of Nevksy and the Moika river stands **Stroganov Palace** (Строгановский дворец – Stroganovsky dvorets; Nevsky 17; http://en.rusmuseum.ru; Fri-Mon and Wed 10am–6pm, Thu 1–9pm), a Baroque masterpiece built by Rastrelli in 1752–4 for the Stroganov family. They lived here until the 1917 revolution. Today, nine rooms have been gloriously restored.

East of the Moika is the pretty **Lutheran Church**, built in the 1830s for the German community (Nevsky 22–24). Made into a vegetable store and then a pool during the Soviet period, it has been returned to the community. On the same (north) side of the street is the landmark

Prince Nevsky

Nevsky prospekt was named after Alexander Nevsky, a prince from Novgorod who routed the Swedes in 1240.

A festive Kazan Cathedral

style moderne former Singer Sewing Machine building (1902–4), now used as shop premises.

The highlight of this stretch of Nevsky is the **Kazan Cathedral** (Собор Казанской Богоматери – Sobor Kazanskoy Bogomateri; Kazanskaya ploshchad 2; www.kazansky-spb.ru; daily; free), commissioned by Paul I in 1801. Designed by the former serf Andrey Voronikhin to resemble St Peter's in Rome, the classical facade has a sweeping 111-metre (364ft) curved colonnade that embraces the square before it, which is, incongruously, a traditional political rallying point and teen hangout. The interior is oddly both spacious and dark, with pink-granite columns and massive chandeliers.

AROUND ARTS SQUARE

The best approach to the lovely **Arts Square** (Площадь Искусств – Ploshchad Iskusstv) is north from Nevsky prospekt along

Mikhailovskaya ulitsa, with the elegant Grand Hotel Europe on the western side and the Philharmonic at the corner of Italyanskaya ulitsa to the east. In an oval park stands a 1957 statue of Pushkin; to the west is the Mussorgsky Opera and Ballet Theatre; straight ahead are the classical buildings of the Mikhailovsky Palace. Behind the palace is the **Mikhailovsky Garden**, surrounded by a particularly fanciful wrought-iron fence. Rossi designed the entire square and garden in the 1820s.

Mikhailovsky Palace was built in 1819–25 by Rossi for the Grand Duke Michael, and made into a museum of Russian art in 1898. The Benois Wing (named after the architect Leonty Benois), to the west of the main building, was constructed in 1914–19 to hold the growing collection (which now numbers over 300,000 pieces of art). Now called the **Russian Museum** ⑯ (Русский музей – Russky muzey; Inzhenernaya ulitsa 4; http://en.rusmuseum. ru; Fri–Sun and Wed 10am–6pm, Mon until 8pm, Thu 1–9pm), it is one of the largest collections of Russian art in the world.

On the first floor, all three wings (main building, Rossi and Benois) display art from the earliest icons to the early 20th century. The second floor is largely dedicated to late 19th- and early 20th-century art, as well as folk art and temporary exhibitions.

Statue of Pushkin in Arts Square

The collection of early religious art contains several magnificent icons by Andrey Rublyov (c.1340–1430). The academic period (starting in 1757 with the opening of the Academy of Arts) is well represented, with particularly interesting portraits by Dmitry Levitsky and fine seascapes by Ivan Ayvazovsky (1817–1900). A rebellion in the Academy in 1863 led to one of Russia's greatest art movements, the

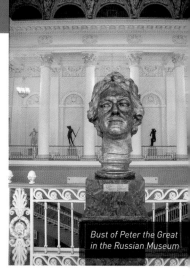

Bust of Peter the Great in the Russian Museum

Wanderers: a group of artists who travelled around the country painting life 'as they saw it' and arranging exhibitions for the masses. Artists like Ilya Repin, Ivan Kramskoy and Nikolay Ge captured Russian life with an almost photographic eye.

In the late 19th century, realism became tempered with lyricism, such as in the landscapes of Isaac Levitan, or romantic historicism, such as in the enormous canvases depicting Russian history by Vasily Surikov, or Russian fairy tales and mythology by Viktor Vasnetsov. Mikhail Vryubel and Nikolay Roerich began to pave the way towards the avant-garde with their impressionistic canvases, and the World of Art painters, like Alexander Benois, rebelled against the social conscience of the realist painters with decorative 'art for art's sake'.

At the turn of the 20th century, the overturning of great artistic canons by the Russian avant-garde paralleled Russia's social and political upheavals. The museum has a particularly fine collection of avant-garde artworks, including paintings by Natalya Goncharova, Kazimir Malevich, Vasily Kandinsky and Marc Chagall.

The collection of folk art is extensive and varied, including toys, embroidery, carvings, ceramics and everyday objects transformed by Russian peasants into fanciful works of art.

Directly to the east of the Russian Museum is the **Museum of Ethnography** ⑰ (Музей этнографии – Muzey etnografii; Inzhenernaya ulitsa 4/1; www.ethnomuseum.ru; Wed–Sat 10am–6pm, Tue until 9pm, Sun 11am–7pm), built in 1900–11. Today it possesses half a million items illustrating every aspect of daily life over the ages across the territory of the former USSR, with particularly fascinating exhibits on traditional life in Siberia and Russia's Far East.

To the northwest of the Russian Museum on the Griboedov Canal is the **Church of the Resurrection of Christ 'On Spilled Blood'** ⑱ (Храм во имя Воскресения Христова «Спаса на крови» – Khram vo imya Voskreseniya Khristova 'Spasa na krovi'; Konyushnaya ploshchad; http://eng.cathedral.ru; Thu–Tue 10.30am–6pm, May–Sept also 6–10.30pm). Built on the spot where Tsar Alexander II was mortally wounded in 1881, its bright colours, patterned cupolas, arcades and arches are a bit of medieval Moscow in the northern capital, while the interior is entirely covered with mosaics. The memorial services for the deceased tsar were held here. During the Soviet period it was a warehouse, but it reopened in 1997 after nearly 30 years of restoration.

To the east of the Russian Museum is **St Michael's Castle** (Михайловский замок – Mikhailovsky zamok; Sadovaya ulitsa 2; http://en.rusmuseum.ru; Fri–Mon and Wed 10am–6pm, Thu 1–9pm), built by Paul I with moats and a drawbridge to protect himself from his enemies. It was completed in 1801 (by architects Vasily Bazhenov and Vincenzo Brenna), and Paul lived here for exactly 40 days before he was murdered in his bed. In 1825 it was made into the Guards Corps of Engineers School (where the writer Fyodor Dostoevsky studied), and it is often called the **Engineer's Castle**. Now part of the Russian Museum, it has several beautifully restored Pauline rooms (including a glittering throne room and marble-filled church), and displays portraits, works of foreign artists who worked in Russia and temporary exhibits.

The Church of the Resurrection of Christ 'On Spilled Blood'

BACK ON NEVSKY PROSPEKT

Between Griboedov Canal and Sadovaya ulitsa stands the great shopping arcade **Gostiny Dvor** ⑲ (Nevsky 35; daily 10am–10pm), built and rebuilt many times over the years to house traders and their wares. The present building was begun by Rastrelli in 1756, completed 1761–85, with the classical porticoes and columns added by Vallin de la Mothe. To the west is the curious **Portik Rusca**, named after architect Luigi Rusca, the entrance to another, less interesting shopping centre. It's located on Dumskaya ulitsa by the striking red **Duma Tower**, built in 1804 as a fire watchtower. The city legislature convened here before the revolution.

Opposite Gostiny Dvor, set back from the road a little, is the pretty blue-and-white neoclassical **Armenian Church** (Nevsky

40–42), built in 1771–80. Also on the north side of the street are two restored pre-revolutionary arcades, the **Passazh** (Nevsky 48) and **Grand Palace** (Nevsky 44).

Between Sadovaya ulitsa and the Fontanka river on the south side of the road is **Ostrovsky Square** (Площадь Островского – Ploshchad Ostrovskovo), named after Alexander Ostrovsky (1823–86), one of Russia's most prolific and beloved playwrights. Built by Rossi in 1818–39, it is one of the city's centres of the arts. Behind the park and statue of Catherine the Great (erected in 1873) is the magnificent **Alexandrinsky** (also called **Pushkin**) **Theatre**. To the west is the **National Public Library**.

On the east side of Ostrovsky Square is the **Anichkov Palace** (Аничков дворец – Anichkov dvorets), first built by Empress Elizabeth for her lover Razumovsky, and then given by Catherine the Great to her lover Potyomkin. The palace was redesigned many times; the present building owes its rather stolid grey classicism to Rossi. It was later used by the heirs to the throne, although Alexander III liked it so much that he and his family continued to live here. It now serves as a Children's Cultural Centre.

The pretty Armenian Church is tucked back from the road

EAST OF ANICHKOV BRIDGE

The **Anichkov Bridge** over the Fontanka river is one of the city's most impressive, adorned at each corner by Pyotr Klodt's sculptures of men taming wild horses. On the southeast side of the Fontanka is the magnificent red Baroque **Beloselsky-Belozersky Palace**, built by Andrey Stakenshneider in 1847–8.

On the east side of the Fontanka, some way north of Nevsky prospekt, stands yet another Baroque palace of yet another fabulously rich noble family. The

> ## Lane of symmetry
>
> To see one of the most perfectly proportioned streets in the world, walk behind Ostrovsky Square to Architect Rossi Street (Улица Зодчего Росси – Ulitsa Zodchevo Rossi). The mirror-image arcaded buildings on either side of the street are 22m (72ft) high, exactly 22m (72ft) apart, and the street itself stretches 220 metres (720ft).

Sheremetev Palace – Museum of Music ❷⓿ (Шереметьевский дворец – Музей музыки – Sheremetevsky dvorets – Muzey muzyki; Nab. reki Fontanki 34; http://theatremuseum.ru; palace rooms Thu–Mon 11am–7pm, Wed 1–9pm, closed last Wed of the month; musical instruments collection Thu–Sun 11am–7pm, Wed 1–9pm), also called the **Fountain House** (Фонтанный дом – Fontanny dom) for the many fountains that once graced the grounds, was built in 1750–5. The Sheremetevs were great patrons of the arts and supported a serf theatre, so it is fitting that the ground floor of the palace is now dedicated to a fantastic collection of musical instruments from every country and virtually every period. The palace rooms are on the first floor.

In the south wing of the palace is the **Anna Akhmatova Museum** (Музей Анны Ахматовой – Muzey Anny Akhmatovoy; entrance at Liteyny prospekt 53; www.akhmatova.spb.ru; Tue, Thu–Sun 10.30am–6.30pm, Wed noon–8pm), where this great poet lived from the mid-1920s until 1952. The museum reconstructs several rooms where she and her third husband, Nikolay Punin, lived, and displays many of her manuscripts, personal possessions and portraits.

The stretch of Nevsky prospekt from the Fontanka to **Ploshchad Vostaniya** (Uprising Square) feels a bit more like a generic big-city street, with international chain hotels, restaurants and upscale stores. The square itself, once a poor district that was the starting point for the 1917 revolution, is just a big roundabout by the Moscow Train Station, with a particularly un-Petersburg array of lurid signage, casinos and cafés.

An interesting museum for literature-lovers is the **Dostoevsky Memorial Museum** (Музей-квартира Ф.М. Достоевского – Muzey-kvartira F.M. Dostoevskovo; Kuznechny pereulok 5/2, Apt 119; www.md.spb.ru; Tue, Thu–Sun 11am–6pm, Wed 1–8pm), south of Nevsky prospekt, where this chronicler of the darker side of St Petersburg lived the last years of his life in middle-class comfort.

⊙ ANNA AKHMATOVA

Anna Akhmatova (1889–1966) was one of the most celebrated poets of the Silver Age. Her first husband, the poet Nikolay Gumilyov, was executed in the first years of Soviet power; her third husband, Punin, was arrested and died in the camps; and her son was imprisoned for many years. Her poems about St Petersburg – the glittering city of her youth and the tragic city of her middle years, when she and her loved ones were hounded by the Soviet authorities – are among the finest poetic expressions of the city. Her celebrated Cubism-inspired portrait by Nathan Altman is in the Russian Museum.

The buildings of the Senate and Synod now house Russia's Constitutional Court

THE ENGLISH QUAY AND SOUTHWEST

The neighbourhoods west and southwest of Palace Square include several magnificent monuments and museums along the Neva river, the city's main cathedral and one of the oldest sections of the city, Kolomna, where quiet residential streets and romantic canals coexist with lavish palaces and the bustle of Theatre Square.

THE ADMIRALTY

To the west of Palace Square is yet another symbol of the city: the imposing **Admiralty ㉑**. In 1704 Peter had a shipyard built here, and in 1718 part of the original building was given over to the naval ministries. In 1806–23, Andreyan Zakharov rebuilt the structure in high classicism, with statues and bas-reliefs celebrating the naval fleet, and a 72-metre (236ft) spire topped

The Bronze Horseman statue in Decembrist Square

with a ship weathervane. Since 1917 it has been a naval college and is closed to the public.

However, you can enjoy views of the building from the pretty **Alexandrovsky Park** ㉒ that stretches from Palace Square to the Manège. Established in 1874 by a botanist, it is filled with rare trees and shrubs, as well as a lovely fountain, busts of writers and a never-ending crowd of dog-walkers, teenage lovers, strolling mothers and tourists.

The park finishes at **Decembrist Square**, named for the ill-fated group of noblemen (see page 18) who staged a rebellion here by the buildings of the **Synod** (of the Russian Orthodox Church) and **Senate** on the west side of the square. These lovely classical buildings, joined with an arch topped by a sculptural group of the goddess of Justice, were built in 1829–36 by Carlo Rossi. The buildings now serve as Russia's Constitutional Court. Next to the Synod and Senate buildings is the **Manège** (Конногвардейский манеж – Konnogvardeysky manezh; Isaakievskaya ploshchad 1; Wed–Sun 10am–6pm), built by Giacomo Quarenghi in 1804–7 to stable and train the imperial horse guards. It is now an exhibition centre.

Near the Neva river bank in Decembrist Square is St Petersburg's most famous monument to Peter the Great, usually called the **Bronze Horseman** ㉓ (Медный всадник – Medny vsadnik). Catherine the Great commissioned Etienne Falconet to design and build it, and after nearly 12 years of artistic quarrelling, it was erected in 1782. While Falconet designed and sculpted the monument, Marie-Anne Collot, Falconet's 18-year-old apprentice, crafted the face of Peter the Great. The monument is dedicated "To Peter I from Catherine II" in Russian and Latin, and depicts Peter the Great trampling the snake of treason under his steed's hoof. The enormous podium of granite the statue rests on is called the Thunder Stone – a stone that had cracked off a cliff when hit by lightning. It weighs over 1,500 tonnes and was hauled here over nine months by 400 men, who moved it about 150 metres (492ft) a day.

THE ENGLISH QUAY AND BEYOND

The stretch of embankment to the west of Decembrist Square is called the **English Quay** (Английская набережная – Angliyskaya naberezhnaya) since it was the original site of the British embassy. It was one of the city's most prestigious addresses, lined with magnificent palaces and mansions, one of which is

⊙ THE BRONZE HORSEMAN

The statue of Peter the Great is called the Bronze Horseman after a poem by Alexander Pushkin written in 1833. In the poem a young man loses his beloved in a great flood, and in his delirium imagines that the statue leaps off the pedestal and chases him through the city. While praising the city and Peter's vision, the poem suggests that the 'little people' suffer from the whims and ambitions of their leaders. All the same, it is traditional for brides and grooms to be photographed by the monument on their wedding day.

now the wonderful **Museum of St Petersburg's History** ㉔ (Музей истории города Санкт Петербурга – Muzey istorii goroda Sankt Peterburga; Angliyskaya nab. 44; www.spbmuseum.ru; Thu–Mon 11am–7pm, Tue 11am–6pm), also called the **Rumyantsev House**, after the owner and museum's founder, Nikolay Rumyantsev. The house is a magnificent backdrop to fascinating exhibitions on the city's history, with emphasis on the blockade and early Soviet period, including recreations of rooms, bunkers, stores, kitchens and other everyday venues, in addition to photos, documents, posters, videos and other memorabilia.

Near the museum is Ploshchad Truda, where the Grand Duke Nikolay had a rather austere palace built in 1853–61, which was eventually turned into a school for noblewomen. The **Nikolaevsky Palace** was given to the trade unions after

The golden dome of St Isaac's, one of the world's largest single-domed churches

the revolution, and remains their headquarters.

Across the square is the timber-storage warehouse called **New Holland** (Новая Голландия – Novaya Gollandiya), founded by Peter the Great in 1719. Rebuilt in 1765, it finally fell out of service and was devastated by fire several years ago.

ST ISAAC'S SQUARE

St Isaac's Square is one of the city's grandest spaces, with the cathedral rising up at one end, the Mariinsky Palace at the other, and a **Monument to Nicholas I** in the centre. The statue was sculpted by Pyotr Klodt in 1859. Images of Faith, Wisdom, Justice and Strength surround the pedestal with scenes from the tsar's reign.

It is positioned in front of the **Mariinsky Palace**, built by Nicholas I for his daughter Maria. Since the late 19th century, the palace has housed municipal councils and administrations. The square is lined with pleasantly proportioned buildings, including the famous **Astoria Hotel**, opened in 1910.

The square is dominated by **St Isaac's Cathedral** ❷❺ (Исаакиевский собор – Isaakievsky sobor; Isaakievskaya ploshchad 1; http://eng.cathedral.ru; Thu–Tue 10.30am–6pm, May–Sept also 6–10.30pm). Named in honour of St Isaac of Dalmatia, whose feast day is celebrated on the day Peter the Great was born, this cathedral was designed and built by Auguste de Montferrand in 1817–58. It is one of the

> ### Golden glory
>
> Over 400kg (882lbs) of gold, 1,000 tonnes of bronze, 16,000kg (32,000lbs) of malachite and 11 sq metres (118 sq ft) of lapis, in addition to marble, porphyry and other stones, were used in the interior of St Isaac's to create columns, statues and mosaics. The 101.5-metre (333ft) high cathedral can hold 14,000 worshippers.

world's largest single-domed churches (the interior dome is 21.8m/70.5ft in diameter), and certainly one of the most lavishly imposing, from its classical exterior with eclectic neo-Renaissance and Baroque ornamentation to its 112 granite columns holding up the pediments.

The church is a typical Petersburgian blend of East and West. It is a traditional Russian cross-plan church, but displays religious arts that were more commonly used in the West, such as the extraordinary stained-glass window of the Resurrected Christ in the sanctuary, the naturalistic frescos, painted by some of the finest artists of the times, and the bronze and gilded statuary in the lavish interior.

⊙ THE MYSTERIOUS MURDER OF RASPUTIN

The last of the Yusupovs to live in the Yusupov Palace were the rather decadent Felix and his wife, Irina, the niece of Tsar Nicholas II. They seem to have had a happy marriage, although even by today's standards it was unconventional: in his autobiography, Felix admitted his pleasure in dressing in women's clothing and partying the night away. Certainly nothing indicated that Felix was destined to play a key role in Russian history. In 1916 he and several accomplices decided to rid Russia of the greatest threat to the empire – Grigory Rasputin. One December night, the conspirators lured Rasputin to the cellar sitting rooms, where they fed him poisoned pastries. When they had no effect, they beat him unconscious. When he ran out of the door, they shot him, and then threw his body in the ice-covered Neva river. Later forensic investigations showed that despite being poisoned, beaten and shot, Rasputin died by drowning.

Sculptures of griffins on the Bank Bridge

KOLOMNA

The area to the southwest of St Isaac's Square between the Moika and Fontanka rivers is called Kolomna, named for the workers from the town of Kolomenskoe who settled here. One of the oldest parts of the city, it remained working class until the mid-19th century. It is a pleasant area for strolling, especially along the winding Moika river and Griboedov Canal. The latter has some of the city's most fanciful bridges, like the gilded griffins of the Bank Bridge (so called because of the nearby bank, now an institute), or the lions of the Lion Bridge at Maly Podyacheskaya ulitsa.

The most famous palace on the Moika River is the **Yusupov Palace** ㉖ (Юсуповский дворец – Yusupovsky dvorets; Nab. reki Moiki 94; www.yusupov-palace.ru; daily 11am–6pm), the only palace in the city that survives with much of its original interior intact. The fabulously wealthy Nikolay Yusupov purchased an older palace on this site in 1830. Over the years, he and his descendants remodelled it to hold their art collection and satisfy their changing tastes. They later added a 'home theatre' that mimics the Mariinsky in miniature. By the time the family fled Russia during the 1917 revolution, the palace was an eclectic mélange of styles, from classicism to Renaissance to rococo to Art Nouveau to Moorish motifs.

⊙ BALLET AND BALLETS RUSSES

Ever since Jean-Baptiste Landé was invited to Russia in 1738 to train dancers for what would become the famed Imperial Ballet School, the Russian school of ballet has produced brilliant dancers, such as Anna Pavlova, Vaslav Nijinksy, Rudolf Nureyev and Mikhail Barishnikov, and the brilliant choreographer Maurius Petipa, who choreographed over 60 ballets over his long life (1818–1910).

After the 1917 revolution, many of the Mariinsky and imperial dancers were eager to leave the country, and were snapped up by Sergey Diaghilev for his Ballets Russes. For his innovative ballets Diaghilev combined such choreographers as Michel Fokine and set-designers like Leon Bakst, Alexander Benois, composers like Igor Stravinsky and dancers like Nijinsky. The troupe, which existed from 1909 to 1929, never performed in Russia.

However, the tradition of imperial training continued under the Soviet regime, languishing in the darkest days of Stalinism, but flourishing once again in the 1960s and 1970s in what was now called the Kirov Theatre. Today the troupe continues to dance under the name Kirov, although the theatre is once more called the Mariinsky.

After the last Yusupovs escaped to Europe and the palace was expropriated by the state, over 1,000 priceless paintings and rare manuscripts were found hidden behind a secret door in Felix's book-lined study. They were eventually distributed to other state museums, but much of the palace remains as it was on the eve of the revolution, with dozens of luxurious and richly decorated public and private rooms

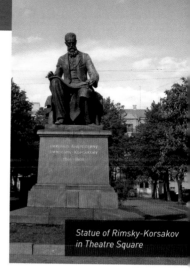

Statue of Rimsky-Korsakov in Theatre Square

open to visitors and often used for concerts and events.

THEATRE SQUARE

In the 18th century the imperial family decided to build a new centre for the performing arts on a square that traditionally held fairs and festivals. Theatre Square is home to the **Mariinsky Theatre** ㉗ and the **Rimsky-Korsakov Conservatory**. The Mariinsky was originally built in 1860, but the present mint-green neo-Renaissance exterior was designed in 1883–96. The interior is a lush, frothy mix of blue, gold and white. The Conservatory, established in 1862 by pianist Anton Rubinshteyn, was completed in 1896.

To the southeast of the square stands the airy blue-and-white **Church of St Nicholas and the Epiphany** (often called Nikolsky Church), one of the city's finest examples of Baroque architecture, set between two canals and behind a leafy square. Nearby is another great religious building, the **Choral Synagogue** (Lermontovsky prospekt 2). In 1869 Alexander II approved construction of the temple, although the house of worship was only completed and consecrated in 1893. The synagogue was designed in the Moorish style by I. Shaposhnikov, but the heavily ornamented interior was designed by Lev Bachman, the first Jewish graduate of the Academy of Arts.

Nearby is the **Railway Museum** ㉘ (Музей железнодорожного транспорта – Muzey zheleznodorozhnovo transporta; Sadovaya ulitsa 50; Sun–Thu 11am–5pm, closed last Thu of the month), specially constructed in 1901–2 (with additions in 1910–11) to hold a collection of photos, documents, models and even a full-size luxury train from the turn of the 20th century. East of here is **Haymarket Square** (Сенная площадь – Sennaya ploshchad), which used to be the heart of lower-class St Petersburg. It has now been reconstructed into a bustling shopping area that evokes nothing of its notorious past.

FURTHER AFIELD

The eastern part of the city, north of Nevsky prospekt between Ploshchad Vostaniya and the Alexander Nevsky Lavra, is a quiet neighbourhood with a few spectacular sights scattered somewhat thinly across the area. To the northeast across the Neva is the Vyborg Side, home to the main memorial cemetery that is the final resting place of the victims of the block-ade. Southern St Petersburg is a part of the city that visitors usually zip through on

Son of Smolny

The most famous former resident of the Smolny neighbourhood is President Vladimir Putin, who grew up in a communal apartment at Baskov pereulok 12.

Smolny Cathedral

their way to and from the airport, but there are several interesting monuments here worth a look, should you have time to spare.

SMOLNY

The Smolny neighbourhood is to the north of Nevsky prospekt as it runs east from Ploshchad Vostaniya. Named for the tar pits (смола – *smola* in Russian) once here, it is a quiet, predominantly residential neighbourhood. In 1748 the Empress Elizabeth planned to build a spectacular Baroque convent, designed by Rastrelli to have a soaring bell tower, cupolas and walls. (The model, which itself took seven years to build, is in the Academy of Arts, see page 40.) All she succeeded in building was some of the convent buildings and the breathtaking blue-and-white confection of the **Smolny Cathedral** ㉙ (Смольный собор – Smolny sobor; Ploshchad Rastrelli 3/1; Fri–Wed 11am–5pm), whose five cupolas rise majestically over the river. Catherine the Great halted the funding and had Ivan Stasov design the interiors in her favourite neoclassical style. Closed as a house of worship after the revolution, the interiors were stripped, and now their disappointingly plain white walls are the backdrop for temporary art exhibitions and concerts.

Nearby is another 'Smolny' – the former **Smolny Institute for Noblewomen**, built by Quarenghi in 1806–8. It was the Bolshevik headquarters right after the revolution, where Vladimir Lenin lived with his wife, Nadezhda Krupskaya. The building is still used as the centre of city government and is not open to visitors.

Not far from the cathedral are the cheerful red-and-white **Kikin's Chambers** (Кикины палаты – Kikiny palaty; Stavropolskaya ulitsa 9), a fine example of Petrine Baroque. Built for one of Peter the Great's companions, Alexander Kikin

Mass at the Holy Trinity Cathedral

(1714–20), they were later used to display the Kunstkamera collection until the museum building was finished on Vasilevsky Island. They are now a music school.

A little further east of the Smolny Cathedral and Institute is the neoclassical **Tauride Palace** (Таврический дворец – Tavrichesky dvorets; Shpalernaya ulitsa 47), built in 1783–9 by Ivan Starov for Catherine the Great as another palace gift for her favourite, Grigory Potyomkin, after his military success in Crimea (once called Tavria). Today the building hosts the Parliamentary Assembly of the CIS (Commonwealth of Independent States) and is not open to the public, but the lovely natural gardens and lake are open for strolling.

> ### Young 'Old Nevsky'
>
> The stretch of Nevsky prospekt from Ploshchad Vostaniya to the Lavra is traditionally called Староневский – Staronevsky, 'Old Nevsky', although it is actually 'younger' than the eastern part of the street.

THE ALEXANDER NEVSKY LAVRA

Nevsky prospekt ends in the west at the **Alexander Nevsky Lavra** ③⓿ (Александро-Невская Лавра – Aleksandro-Nevskaya Lavra; daily 6am–8pm; free), founded in 1710 by Peter the Great in honour of Alexander Nevsky. Reached through a gate and path that is lined with the poor and infirm begging for alms, this active monastery seems to exist in a different time and place. The oldest church in the monastery is the red-and-white **Church of the Annunciation**, built by Trezzini in 1717–22. The main church, the **Holy Trinity Cathedral**, was built in the neoclassical style by Ivan Starov in 1776–90, with magnificent golden Royal Gates leading to the sanctuary. A silver-and-gold reliquary with the remains of Alexander Nevsky is to the right of the altar. In 1993 they were returned to the church from the Museum of Religion and Atheism, where they had been kept after the revolution. The monastery was closed from 1922 to 1956, when only one church was allowed to open for services. The monastery was revived in 1994.

Adjoining the monastery are cemeteries where St Petersburg's most important citizens were once buried, a kind of St Petersburg Père Lachaise. In 1932, after the monastery was closed, the state renamed the cemeteries the **Museum of Urban Sculpture** (Музей городской скульптуры – Muzey gorodskoy skulptury; Fri–Wed 11am–5pm) and moved many artistically valuable gravestones here. Among the people interred in these leafy and pleasant grounds are Mikhail Lomonosov, Carlo Rossi, Giacomo Quarenghi, Fyodor Dostoevsky, Mikhail Glinka, Marius Petipa and Pyotr Tchaikovsky.

Anyone who loves the decorative arts should trek south along the Neva to the **Imperial Porcelain Factory Museum** ㉛ (Музей императорского фарфорового завода – Muzey imperatorskovo farforovovo zavoda; Prospekt Obukhovskoy oborony 151; www.hermitagemuseum.org; Tue, Thu, Sat, Sun 10.30am–6pm, Wed and Fri until 9pm; free first Thu of the month; Lomonosovskaya metro), called the Lomonosov Factory during the Soviet years and now a branch of the Hermitage. Opened in 1744, the factory produced porcelain for the imperial family, and its museum halls display 250 years of porcelain masterpieces. The most impressive piece is a large 'Biscuit Bouquet' (unglazed fired porcelain) made in 1850. Every petal is so delicate and lifelike that it's hard to believe it was crafted in clay by human hands.

VYBORG SIDE

The area north of the eastern part of St Petersburg on the other side of the Neva, called the Vyborg Side, has a few pockets of pretty residential areas amidst a great deal of industrial urban landscape. It is famous for the **Finland Station** (Ploshchad Lenina 6), where Lenin arrived after 17 years of plotting revolution in European exile, and made his renowned speech on top of an armoured train. The station itself is a grim Soviet replacement, but there is a legendary statue of Lenin in the middle of the square, now surrounded by all the detritus of the capitalist Russia that the leader of the proletariat would have despised.

The main reason to visit the Vyborg Side is the cemetery of mass graves where the victims of the blockade were buried. **Piskaryovskoe Cemetery** ㉜ (Пискарёвское мемориальное кладбище – Piskaryovskoe memorialnoe kladbishche; Prospekt Nepokoryonnikh 72; daily 9am–6pm, until 9pm in summer; free; metro Lesnaya or Ploshchad Muzhestva) was the

place where over 500,000 bodies were buried in mass graves from 1941–3. In 1960, the memorial complex was redesigned with two memorial halls and the grand mourning figure of Mother Russia by Vera Isaeva and Robert Taurit. On the wall behind it is a poem by Olga Berggolts, which ends with the oft-quoted phrase: 'No one and nothing is forgotten.' Music is broadcast throughout the cemetery, making every visit to this place a pilgrimage.

Piskaryovskoe memorial

SOUTHERN SUBURBS

Joseph Stalin, allegedly revolted by the imperial and aristocratic city centre of St Petersburg, hatched a grandiose plan to move the centre south to Moskovsky prospekt. He managed to initiate work on the enormous 'Stalinist classical' **House of Soviets** (Moskovsky prospekt 2/2), which was completed after the war, but thankfully his grand plan was never brought to fruition.

There are three monuments here of considerable historical interest. The enormous 12-columned **Moscow Triumphal Arch** at Ploshchad Moskovskie Vorota was built by Vasily Stasov in 1838 to commemorate the Russo-Turkish War. Another triumphal arch further west, the **Narva Triumphal Gate** (Ploshchad Stachek), was designed by Quarenghi and erected in 1814 to commemorate victory over Napoleon's armies. It was redesigned and built by Vasily Stasov in 1827–34, topped by a magnificent sculptural group of the goddess of Victory in her chariot led by six horses, sculpted by Pyotr Klodt.

A monument at Ploshchad Pobedy commemorates the **Defenders of Leningrad**. This huge sculptural group includes 34 bronze figures. Under the monument is a **museum** about the blockade (Монумент героическим защитникам Ленинграда – Monument geroicheskim zashchitnikam Leningrada; http://www.spbmuseum.ru; Thu–Mon 10am–6pm, Tue until 5pm), which has 900 bronze sheets chronicling the siege, lit by 900 bronze lamps, as a metronome beats out the city's heartbeat, just as it did on the radio during the blockade.

The southern part of the city also has one extraordinary religious monument – the **Chesma Church** (Чесменская церковь – Chesmenskaya tserkov; Ulitsa Lensoveta 12; www.chesma.spb.ru; daily 10am–7pm; free), built 1777–80 by Yuti Felten and named in honour of the Battle of Çesme in the Russo-Turkish War. The only neo-Gothic church in the city, its red facade with thin vertical lines of white moulding, tower-like cupolas and unusual shape, are an aesthetic shock in this otherwise undistinguished neighbourhood.

PALACE EXCURSIONS

The 'necklace' of palaces that ring the city are even more magnificent than the imperial domiciles in the city centre. Almost all of them were occupied and destroyed by the German armies in World War II, although most of the furnishings, art and fittings were evacuated in advance. What you see today is a double miracle: the incredible beauty of the original buildings and parks, and the astonishing work of thousands of restorers who have been bringing this beauty back to life from the ashes and rubble.

The Grand Palace at Peterhof

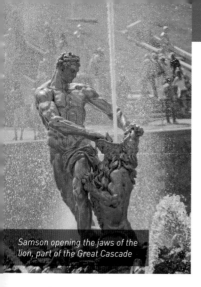
Samson opening the jaws of the lion, part of the Great Cascade

PETERHOF

In 1709 Peter the Great began to build a palace overlooking the Gulf of Finland. He then changed his vision after visiting Versailles in 1717. **Peterhof** ㉝ (Петеров; www.peter hofmuseum.ru; Grand Palace Tue–Sun 10.30am–7pm, closed last Tue of the month; other buildings closed on various days; all buildings open Fri–Sun; fountains open May–Sept) was built and rebuilt many times, most notably under the luxury-loving Elizabeth and her court architect Rastrelli. Parts of the **Grand Palace** (first built in 1714–25 by the architects Braunstein, Zemtsov and Le Blond, and then rebuilt and expanded by Rastrelli in 1745–55) are still under partial restoration, but the dozens of restored rooms, with their original art, furnishing and chandeliers in place, are a truly remarkable spectacle. Also in the grounds is the charming **Monplaisir** (1714–22), the small 'cottage' where Peter the Great preferred to stay, the **Marly Palace**, the neo-Gothic **Cottage Palace** (1826–9) and the **Hermitage** (1721–5) – a pink-and-white confection surrounded by a moat. This was a private dining room with a table that could be raised and lowered from the kitchen below, fully set and covered with food and drink.

These palaces are set on nearly 600 hectares (1,500 acres) of formal and landscaped parks, filled with fountains. The masterpiece is the **Great Cascade**: 64 fountains, 142 water jets and 37 gold statues, including the magnificent **Statue of Samson** opening the jaws of the lion (an allegory for Peter's victory over the Swedes). There are 144 fountains in the park, ranging from the magnificent to the silly – like hidden fountains set off by footsteps. They are fed by 40km (25 miles) of pipes without a single pump – a unique feat of aquatic engineering.

TSARSKOE SELO

In the 18th century, about 25km (16 miles) to the south of St Petersburg, there was a Finnish estate called Saarimois, or Sarskaya myza in Russian, which meant 'farmstead on a promontory'. After going through several hands, the property was given to Catherine I, the wife of Peter the Great, who had a stone cottage and formal gardens built. When her daughter the Empress Elizabeth inherited it, she commissioned Rastrelli to build an enormous summer palace there, named the **Catherine Palace** (www.tzar.ru; Wed–Mon June–Aug noon–6.45pm, shorter hours rest of the year) in honour of her mother. She spent 1.2 million roubles on the palace and parks, including over 100kg (220lbs) of gold on the interior and exterior ornamentation. The second Catherine ('the Great') had Charles Cameron build neoclassical additions to

The golden domes of the Catherine Palace

The Amber Room

the original Baroque structure. Over the centuries, the village name Sarskaya myza changed to Tsarskoe selo (the tsar's village).

Today, much of Rastrelli's robin-egg-blue-and-gold palace has been restored, including the spectacular **Great Hall**, lined with mirrors and windows covered with carved, gilded wood, and the 'eighth wonder of the world', the recreated **Amber Room**.

The expansive grounds of the palace (nearly 560 hectares/1,400 acres) include the original formal gardens and the natural **Landscaped Gardens** commissioned by Catherine the Great, with beautiful buildings, pavilions and sculptures nestled into the gentle hills and around the **Great Pond**. One of the most beautiful neoclassical structures in Russia is the **Cameron Gallery**, designed by Charles Cameron in 1783–7. Here, Catherine held formal dinners by the rows of busts of Greek and Roman heroes (and one Russian – the scientist and philosopher Mikhail Lomonosov).

Attached to the Catherine Palace by an arch is the **Lycée** (Sadovaya ulitsa 2; Wed–Mon 10.30am–6pm, closed last Fri of the month), founded in 1811 to provide classical education to the upper classes. The Lycée has been restored and is a museum showing the classrooms, rather Spartan dormitory rooms and imposing public halls of Russia's foremost academy. Russia's premier poet, Alexander Pushkin, studied here and then lived in the town with his wife in a small wooden cottage that is now the charming **Pushkin Dacha Museum** (Мемориальный музей-дача А.С.Пушкина – Memorialny muzey-dacha A.S. Pushkina; Pushkinskaya ulitsa 2/19; Wed–Sun 10.30am–6pm, closed last Fri of the

⊙ THE AMBER ROOM

The original Amber Room was created in 1701–9 for the Charlottenburg Palace of Friedrich I of Prussia. In 1716, Peter the Great admired it and, as legend has it, bought it in exchange for 55 grenadier soldiers and his personal drinking mug. The room was shipped to St Petersburg and first installed in the Winter Palace, but Empress Elizabeth had it moved to the Catherine Palace and invited German and Russian artisans to enlarge the panels to fit the more spacious room. Over 6 tonnes of intricately carved, brilliantly coloured amber covered 55 sq metres (592 sq ft).

Because the fragile and brittle amber could not be moved easily, before World War II Russian curators covered the walls with wallpaper to hide the treasure from the German army. This ruse did not work, and when the palace came under attack, the Germans disassembled it in 36 hours and shipped it out. That was the last anyone saw of it, despite hundreds of attempts to find it. The only original piece found was one of the Florentine mosaic inlays, which surfaced in 1997.

In 1979 Russian artisans began to rebuild the magnificent room using old photographs and drawings as their guide. It was dedicated and opened in 2003 during the celebration of St Petersburg's 300th anniversary. A share of the restoration work was funded through donations from Germany.

month). During the Soviet period, the town was renamed Pushkin in honour of the poet.

PAVLOVSK

In 1777, Catherine the Great gave her son Paul the lovely land at **Pavlovsk** (Павловск; Ulitsa Revolyutsii 20; www.pavlovsk museum.ru; 10am–6pm, closed first Mon of the month) by the Slavyanka river, to commemorate the birth of her grandson and future tsar, Alexander I. **The Palace**, many of the pavilions and the landscaped English-style park were largely designed by Charles Cameron. The palace is a masterpiece of neoclassicism, with a 64-columned dome dominating its graceful facade. Today it is filled with much of the original furniture and art (including some from Gatchina, another Pauline palace), making it one of the most interesting residences for lovers of the applied arts.

The **Park** in which the palace is set is particularly beautiful, with rolling hills, ponds and the winding river Slavyanka. Originally it was filled with galleries for songbirds and gardens of roses, Paul's wife Mariya's favourite flower. Of particular interest are the **Apollo Colonnade**, designed by Cameron in 1782–3 as an artfully created ruin, and the **Temple to Friendship**, which was commissioned by Mariya in 1780 to ensure

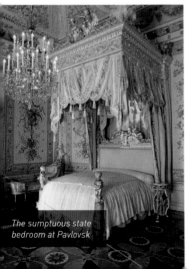

The sumptuous state bedroom at Pavlovsk

warm relations with her mother-in-law, the Empress Catherine. Today Pavlovsk continues to celebrate Mariya's love of roses with an annual rose festival in June.

> **Milestones**
>
> On the roads leading out of St Petersburg are stone markers called вёрсты – *vyorsty*, marking each *vyorst* (1.6km or about 1 mile) from the capital.

STRELNYA: THE CONSTANTINE PALACE

Strelnya (Thu–Tue 10am–6pm by appointment or tour only; see page 122) was the first site Peter the Great contemplated for his Russian Versailles. In 1721 he began to build a **Palace**, and then abandoned it when he decided on the site at Peterhof. It had many owners before the revolution, including the Grand Dukes Constantine (younger sons of Paul and Nicholas I). After the revolution, it was used by many organisations, destroyed by the German armies, partially rebuilt and then abandoned after a fire in 1986. In 2001 the Russian government decided it was just what was needed for the Group of Eight summit, and in a mere 18 months the entire palace and grounds were reconstructed, complete with helicopter pad and a hotel of 20 cottages for the visiting dignitaries.

Today it is not a museum, but an official governmental residence (which means a security detail troops along with the tourists). The fun of it is seeing the spectacularly reconstructed palace rooms, both grand and intimate, where the presidents of the eight great world powers and other leaders held their formal and informal meetings. Of particular interest is the **Belvedere Room**, designed like a cosy ship's cabin at the top of the palace, where Mr Bush and Mr Putin chatted, and the Dutch-style **Kitchen** down below, where Mr Putin entertained such leaders as Italian Premier Berlusconi and German Chancellor Shröder.

The Church of the Resurrection
of Christ 'On Spilled Blood'

WHAT TO DO

St Petersburg by night is as captivating as St Petersburg by day. For lovers of the classical performing arts, the city offers so much dance, music and theatre in such breath-taking venues that it will be hard to decide where to go. For visitors with more contemporary musical tastes, there are a plethora of clubs, bars and concert halls with everything from reggae to techno. You can take a respite from museums by shopping for bargains (still to be had) in pre-revolutionary arcades or at street stalls, or stroll through some of the city's parks, take in a football game or indulge in the city's best way to sightsee – a boat tour that cruises the canals. If you come with children, you will find the city relatively child-friendly and offering a surprising range of activities for the kids.

ENTERTAINMENT AND NIGHTLIFE

Performances and concerts usually begin at 7pm, precluding a pre-theatre dinner, but there are stands in virtually all the theatres and concert halls that open before the performance and during intermissions selling sandwiches, drinks and pastries. Coats and large bags must be checked in. Tickets can be purchased at the box offices at the theatres, at theatre kiosks around the city or through hotel service desks. Note that tickets for the Mariinsky are only sold at the theatre box offices, the Central Railway Ticket Office and the well-marked outlet on the second floor of Gostiny Dvor (the southeast corner where all the tour buses gather). Obviously avoid buying from touts who usually furtively sell tickets at the prime venues.

OPERA, DANCE AND MUSIC

The classical performing arts, nurtured, supported and sponsored by the imperial families for centuries, continue to maintain the highest levels of artistry and professionalism. The Mariinsky Theatre (Teatralnaya ploshchad 1; www.mariinsky.ru; tel: 812-326 4141) and its rather incongruous modern glass-and-steel sister venue, is home to the famous Kirov Ballet (the troupe kept the more familiar Soviet name), under the artistic direction of Valery Gergiev. Across the street, the Conservatory (Teatralnaya ploshchad 3; http://istud.conservatory.ru; tel: 812-571 0506) holds some of the best concerts in the city. The Mussorgsky Opera and Ballet (Ploshchad Iskusstv 1; www.mikhailovsky.ru; tel: 812-595 4305) and Philharmonic (Mikhailovskaya ulitsa 2; www.philharmonia.spb.ru; tel: 812-710 4290) also have high-quality performances. The lovely Academic Capella (Nab. reki Moiki 20; http://capella-spb.ru; tel: 812-314 1058) holds concerts and festivals.

Some of the most divine musical evenings are to be had in former palaces and cathedrals. The airy Smolny Cathedral is a concert hall (Ploshchad Rastrelli 3/1; tel: 812-577 1421) that holds many concerts of religious music. And the concerts in the Hermitage Theatre, Yusupov and Anichkov palaces are as much a celebration of the famous halls as the music itself.

Queue tip

In the large theatres and halls you can rent opera glasses from the cloakroom attendant – even if you don't need them, take them. People returning binoculars get to jump to the head of the queue to get their coats.

THEATRE

St Petersburg was the theatrical centre of the empire until Stanislavsky and Nemerovich-Danchenko changed the world of drama with their Moscow Art Theatre, after which the theatrical lights seemed to burn a bit more brightly in the southern capital. But theatregoing is still a joy in St Petersburg, even if you can't understand much: the halls themselves, as well as the rituals of champagne and smoked salmon during the intermissions, make the entire experience a theatrical event. For classic theatre, try the Pushkin Theatre

Mariinsky Theatre ballet

(more commonly known as the Alexandrinsky) or the Bolshoy Dramatic Theatre. More innovative drama can be found at Lev Dodin's Maly Dramatic Theatre.

NIGHTLIFE

Russians are jazz fiends. Ever since the first jazz band appeared in 1922, they have been tapping their feet to excellent jazz, both home-grown and imported. The classic jazz site in St Petersburg is the Jazz Philharmonic (Zagorodny prospekt 27), or the JFC Jazz Club (Shpalernaya ulitsa 33). For old-time rock and roll fans, St Petersburg was once the hub of the underground rock scene, and no performance by the groups DDTor Aquarium should be missed.

The club scene changes frequently, so be sure to check local listings for the latest trendy hang-out. Long-standing favourites are Avrora (Pirogovskaya naberezhnaya 5/2), Griboedov Bunker (Voronezhskaya ulitsa 2A) or Belgrad (Dumskaya ulitsa 9). If you feel like a real party, drop by one of the two Purga bars (Nab. reki Fontanki 11); the waiting staff tend to dress up as animals, and every night at midnight everyone celebrates New Year. Casinos often have top pop-music acts at the weekend in addition to the usual risqué forms of entertainment. Most clubs have an entry fee and some have face control, where entry is limited according to your dress, demeanour and even your ostensible wealth; casinos usually require a minimum purchase of chips to enter.

SHOPPING

St Petersburg still doesn't have truly great boutique shopping, but there are plenty of arcades and shops where you can find good bargains, interesting wares and plenty of souvenirs. Just be sure to buy only contemporary crafts and mementoes: any antiques, if actually the real deal, must be first cleared by the Ministry of Culture before export, and Soviet military medals cannot be taken out of the country at all.

Honeyed promises

If you think honey is sweet, clear, syrupy stuff, think again. Or better yet, step into a store or market selling Russian honey. You'll see dozens of varieties, from transparent acacia honey to opaque brown buckwheat honey, which is slightly bitter. Each kind has its own flavour and special properties, from helping you fall asleep to cleansing your insides.

WHAT TO BUY

Amber and semi-precious stones. Amber from the Baltic Sea comes in many colours: transparent yellow, creamy gold, dark amber or even white or green. Semi-precious stones from the Urals and Siberia are also priced well and are lovely, especially malachite, lapis

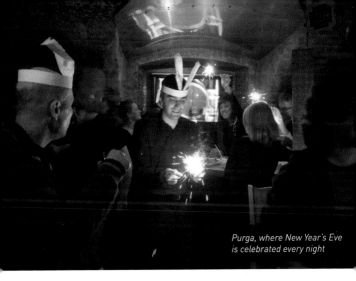

Purga, where New Year's Eve is celebrated every night

lazuli and charoite (a purple stone discovered in the late 20th century by the river Chara).

Ceramics, porcelain and crystal. The Imperial Factory still makes some of the finest bone china in the world, which can be purchased at excellent prices. Russian crystal is also high-quality and a good bargain. Blue-and-white ceramics from Gzhel are another traditional craft.

Food and drink. Try some flavoured varieties of vodka or a jar of good caviar (best purchased in one of the shops in Gostiny Dvor, and never on the street). Russian chocolates are richer than Western varieties; look for Korkunov or candies from the local Krupskaya chocolate factory.

Fur. St Petersburg has ample fur stores selling locally designed coats, jackets and hats made from Russian pelts, as well as cheaper goods from Italy, Turkey or Greece. The best hats are fox, mink, sable and karakul, and the best time to buy is in the summer, when prices are low. Check the seams to be sure they are tight, and scrunch the hat to be sure the fur pops up (if it doesn't, the fur may be dried out or old).

Lacquer boxes. Although lacquer boxes seem to be an age-old craft, they were actually begun in the Soviet period when icon-painters transferred their techniques to making these small boxes. The towns of Palekh, Mstera, Fedoskino and Kholuy each have their own styles. To be sure you are buying the real thing, run your finger over the edges of the painting. If it isn't smooth, the image may be an appliqué.

Linen and woollens. St Petersburg has a number of shops selling fine linen – both bed and table linen and clothing. You can also find good lace and embroidery. Paisley scarves come in a plethora of colours and designs, but be sure to ask if they are Russian-made. If you come from a cold climate, look for hand-knitted angora socks, sweaters and scarves.

Soviet memorabilia. There is plenty of Soviet kitsch for sale, from army surplus wares to old banners. Be sure not to buy any military medals or badges, which cannot be exported. Modern watches, flasks and camouflage gear are popular souvenirs but these days a lot of Soviet-era knick-knacks are actually imitations made in China.

Toys and dolls. The matryoshka (nesting) doll is said to have been invented in a small town outside Moscow, but it has spread across the country as its most identifiable souvenir. Cost is determined by the number of dolls and the quality of the painting. Another good bargain is carved wooden toys and Christmas tree decorations.

WHERE TO SHOP

Artisan and souvenir markets. The main outdoor crafts market in the city is by the Church 'On Spilled Blood', where

Gostiny dvor, the city's shopping hub

hundreds of vendors operate from dawn to dusk (and nearly all night during the White Nights). Artists sell their canvases in front of St Catherine's Church (Nevsky prospekt 32–34), and another group does caricatures on Ploshchad Ostrovskovo.

Pre-revolutionary department stores. The city's shopping Mecca remains Gostiny Dvor (Nevsky prospekt 35), where there are hundreds of little stores selling everything from honey to fur coats, toasters and shampoo. The glass-roofed Passazh (Nevsky prospekt 48) and snazzy Grand Palace (Nevsky prospekt 44) are now classy shopping arcades, with some traditional Russian wares amidst foreign brands.

Gift and souvenir shops. The city boasts many souvenir shops, all of which tend to have the same selection of crafts. The most interesting are Naslediye (several outlets at Nevsky prospect: 11, 22, 29, 32 and 57) and Nevsky Souvenir (throughout the city). Amber & Art (Nab. reki Moiki 1) has an enormous and varied selection

Christmas market

of amber in all colours. The Gallery of Glass (Ulitsa Lomonosova 1/28) offers hand-blown crystal and an interesting assortment of handmade glass, ceramic and enamel art. The factory store (Prospekt Obukhovskoy oborony 151) can't be beaten for good prices on imperial porcelain. The store has an enormous selection of china (which they can ship for you), including the famous Cobalt Net service (designed in 1950 and based on an imperial pattern). If you have deep pockets, you can order an entire imperial service or have their artists design your own family china. Galereya Kukol (Ulitsa Bolshaya Morskaya 53/8) sells handmade puppets and dolls, as well as exhibiting museum-quality pieces. Military paraphernalia can be found at the packed shop on Ulitsa Sadovaya 26.

Books and electronic goods. Dom Knigi (Nevsky prospekt 28) has large selections of art books and posters. The Anglia bookshop (Nab. reki Fontanki 38) has a good variety of books in English on Russia, as well as paperbacks, maps and guidebooks. The funky art shop at Pushkinskaya 10 (entrance from Ligovsky prospekt 53) has a great collection of art books, posters and cards, with an emphasis on non-conformist art and Soviet kitsch. Dom Knigi and many shops in Gostiny Dvor also have a large selection of films, as well as video games and music. Discs sold on the street, in kiosks and at the electronics markets are generally pirated. The Fonoteka store (Ulitsa Marata 28) offers a wide selection of rare CDs, vinyl records and DVDs.

Art galleries. St Petersburg's art world has not reassumed the glory of the pre-revolutionary years or risen to the hype of Moscow's, but the lively underground art world of the Soviet years has morphed into an original, interesting and lively art scene. For hard-core, non-conformist art, visit Ulitsa Pushkinskaya 10 (entrance at Ligovsky prospekt 53). The buildings were originally taken over by squatters in the late 1980s and are now filled with floor after floor of apartments, galleries, studios and places where artistic happenings are still happening. It is also filled with witty graffiti and extravagantly dressed and coifed young people. For something a bit more down-to-earth, the friendly and savvy SPAS Gallery (Nab. reki Moiki 93) is a small gallery that has been representing a variety of artists for the last ten years. Another friendly salon with a wide variety of art (from the 1920s) is Sol Art, located in the Stieglitz Museum (Solyanoy pereulok 13–15). The Marina Gisich Gallery (Nab. reki Fontanki 121/13), Borey Art Gallery (Liteyny prospekt 58) and D137 Art Club (Ulitsa Rubinshteyna 15–17) are considered the city's cutting-edge art dealers. All dealers arrange export permissions (and shipping); works purchased on the street for under US$100 are usually not questioned at customs (although customs officials exercise considerable discretion), so ask for a receipt, even handwritten, for any art you purchase.

> **Your best price?**
>
> Bargaining is acceptable within limits: street vendors will round down the price or give a discount for a large purchase. But don't expect to get much more than 10–20 percent off the asking price.

OUTDOOR ACTIVITIES

BOAT TRIPS

St Petersburg should be seen at least once from the water. During the warm weather there are canal tours with booking offices and boarding points by Nevsky prospekt on the Moika, Griboedov Canal and Fontanka. Larger boats on the Neva (booking office and boarding by the Winter Palace) offer tours and a great and comfortable route to Peterhof palace. Water taxis can also be found by Nevsky prospekt; they can either take you quickly from point A to point B, or be hired for a private tour of the canals and rivers.

⊙ RIVERS AND CANALS

The three main waterways on the palace side of the Neva river – the Moika river, Griboedov Canal and Fontanka river – are all crossed by magnificent bridges: some wide enough for traffic and pedestrians, some so narrow they can only be crossed in single file, and all decorated with magnificent wrought-iron railings, statuary and ornamentation.

If you cruise the Moika (or walk along its banks) from the Hermitage to the south, the first one you will see is the Singer's Bridge, with its intricately formed railings. This was once painted bright yellow, and further south were other bridges painted red and blue. Near the Yusupov Palace is the Lantern Bridge with lamp-posts styled as treble clefs. Further south, near the Kryukov Canal and the ghostly New Holland is the Kisses Bridge, named for a tavern that once stood nearby, which presumably offered more than pub grub to its patrons.

The most beautiful bridges over the Griboedov Canal are south of Nevsky prospekt: the black-and-gold griffins on the Bank Bridge by Ulitsa Lomonosova and the white stone lions on the Lion Bridge by Lviny pereulok, not far from the Mariinsky Theatre. On the Fontanka River, one of the most intricate bridges is the Bridge of St Panteleimon, by the Summer Garden. Its gold-and-black lanterns

A boat trip is a must

are topped with double-headed eagles, and it was named for the red early-Baroque Church of St Panteleimon (dating to 1722, one of the oldest extant churches in the city) on nearby Ulitsa Pestelya. At the far southern end of the river, where it is crossed by Lomonosovsky prospekt, is the magnificent Egyptian Bridge, with its black-and-gold sphinxes. It was built in the early 19th century at the height of the city's fascination with ancient Egypt.

FOOTBALL AND BATH HOUSES

Everybody in St Petersburg loves the Zenit football team (www.fc-zenit.ru), even the police, since the crime statistics go down every time there is an important match. You can get a ticket at the Petrovsky stadium box office, through kiosks or from your hotel. If you are a hockey fan, the local team, SKA, plays from September to June at the Yubileyny Sports Palace.

Alternatively you can try that quintessential Russian relaxation technique: a visit to a bathhouse (баня – banya). You can rent an entire facility for an evening (ask at your hotel), or visit the Yamskie bath house (Ulitsa Dostoevskovo 9), which offers a full range of pampering delights in old-world elegance.

CHILDREN'S ST PETERSBURG

St Petersburg is great for kids – there are plenty of ships and cannons to clamber on, not to mention creepy squiggly things in the Kunstkamera and trick fountains at Peterhof.

Bolshoy Puppet Theatre (Ulitsa Nekrasova 10; tel: 812-273 6672). Established in 1931, this theatre has nearly 20 different shows.

Demmeni Marionette Theatre (Nevsky prospekt 52; tel: 812-571 1900). This puppet theatre is the oldest in Russia, founded in 1918. It later merged with another puppet theatre directed by the brilliant puppet master Yevgeny Demmeni. The theatre's repertoire consists of 15 pieces in various styles and genres, based on the works of both Russian and foreign authors.

Leningradsky Zoo (Alexandrovsky park 1; www.spbzoo.ru; tel: 812-232 8260). Old Russian zoos are only slowly being redesigned for maximum animal comfort. This zoo was opened in 1865 and is home to nearly 2,000 creatures.

Puppet Fairy-Tale Theatre (Moskovsky prospekt 12; tel: 812-388 0031). Another top theatre with puppets and actors in flamboyant costumes.

St Petersburg State Circus (Nab. reki Fontanki 3; www.circus.spb.ru; tel: 812-570 5198). The St Petersburg Circus – and with it many of the renowned Russian circus arts – was founded in 1877 in the first stone circus building in Russia. The founder was an Italian circus performer and trainer, Gaetano Ciniselli. Over the decades the acts have become more spectacular.

CALENDAR OF EVENTS

Since the fall of communism many church and pagan holidays and festivals have been revived. There are also various arts festivals held in St Petersburg.

Christmas and New Year The Arts Square Winter Musical Festival, held at the Philharmonic.

February The week before Lent is Maslenitsa (Butter Week), a wild celebration of bliny-eating and festivities, celebrated around the city and in suburban parks. Bucket loads of alcoholic beverages are drunk and there are usually games and competitions.

March–April The Mariinsky's annual ballet festival.

May The Peterhof fountains are opened with a bang on the first weekend. City Day (last weekend) with city-wide festivities, outdoor concerts and special events at the Peter and Paul Fortress.

May–June The Musical Collection Festival held at the Philharmonic.

May–July The White Nights Festival organised by the city administration, including the Stars of the White Nights performance and other classical opera, music and ballet shows at the Mariinsky theatre, as well as the traditional Scarlet Sails water show and fireworks. During the White Nights of June, crowds also gather at 2am on both sides of the River Neva, near the Hermitage, to watch the raising of the drawbridges to allow seagoing vessels to pass.

June In Tsarskoe selo there is an annual carnival on the last weekend in June.

July Navy Day (first Sunday after 22 July) fills the Neva with ships, boats and submarines.

August The Singing World International Choral Festival.

September The Peterhof fountains are at the centre of a spectacular dance, music, light and fireworks extravaganza (second weekend). The new performing arts season begins in September, usually with a number of high-profile premieres. The Sergey Kuryokhin International Festival is named after and in honour of the talented avant-garde composer and musician who died in 1996.

EATING OUT

When Peter the Great moved his court north to St Petersburg, his noblemen brought with them their customs, culture and cuisine. Although the city is much farther north, the displaced Muscovites had at their disposal the same root vegetables, game and fish, and used their recipes from home. Over the centuries this traditional peasant-hearty Russian cuisine was modified by European cuisines, particularly French, which was reflected in richer and more complex dishes – notably buttery and creamy pastries.

Despite the stagnation of the Soviet era, St Petersburg still has a fine tradition of pre-revolutionary restaurants and an elegant European-inspired cuisine. Today you can find cuisine from virtually every country and nation on earth, but the best restaurants are celebrating their native cuisine with traditional and updated recipes in settings that have been restored to their previous grandeur.

WHERE TO EAT

Although there are a variety of good restaurants all over the city, many are concentrated near the major squares, and particularly along and around Nevsky prospekt. Restaurants specifically catering to foreign tourists are usually below-par, but virtually every café or restaurant has an English menu.

Look for signs for the бизнес-ланч (business lunch); these fixed-price meals of starter, soup, main and a drink are normally a real bargain and might be served until 3pm or 4pm. For a quick and cheap bite to eat, the city's many bliny shops can't be beaten. Stop in a bar café for some good local beer (пиво – *pivo*) and a traditional order of boiled crayfish (раки – *raki*) or shrimp (креветки – *krevetki*), or a slice or two of garlic toast (сухарики – *sukhariki*).

WHEN TO EAT

Breakfast is usually served from about 7am to noon. The lunch hour stretches from noon to 4pm, and dinner is usually served from 6 to 11pm (sometimes until the last customer), although most restaurants only get crowded after 7 or 8pm. All day long you can stop in a coffee shop (кофейня – *kofeynya*) for coffee, tea and sweet and savoury treats, or a bliny shop for pancakes with traditional fillings (икра – caviar, or селёдка – herring), fusion fillings (wild mixtures of, say, chicken and pineapple) or sweetened with jam (варенье – *varene*).

BREAKFAST

Russian breakfasts (завтрак – *zavtrak*) are varied and include dairy products, pastries and other delicious treats made of

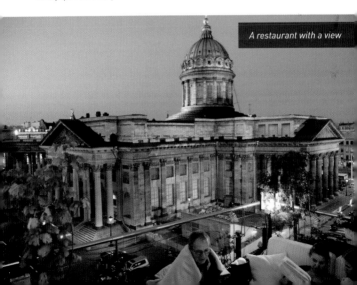

A restaurant with a view

dough, a variety of porridges, eggs, as well as an assortment of smoked meats and fish, and sometimes cucumbers, tomatoes and other vegetables. Porridge (каша – *kasha*) is usually eaten with jam or sour cream (сметана – *smetana*). Cheese pancakes (сырники – *syrniki*) and bliny (блины) are also served with sour cream, jam or condensed milk. The dairy tray usually includes cottage cheese (творог – *tvorog*), yoghurt (йогурт – *iogurt*) and kefir (кефир – *kefir*). In most restaurants or hotel cafés, you can find hard-boiled eggs (варёные яйца – *varyonye yaytsa*), omelette (омлет – *omlet*) or fried eggs (яичница – *yaichnitsa*). There will always be an ample supply of bread, both white (булка – *bulka*) and dark (чёрный – *chyorny*).

LUNCH AND SUPPER

Russians have traditionally eaten their largest meal in the middle of the day. Lunch (обед – *obed*) usually consists of a starter (закуски – *zakuski*) and/or salad (салат – *salat*), soup (суп – *sup*), a main course (второе – *vtoroe*) and dessert (сладкое – *sladkoe*). The evening meal (ужин – *uzhin*) is often a much lighter accompaniment to tea, like open sandwiches (бутерброд – *buterbrod*). Today the demands of work make the full three-course lunch impossible for many, and evenings are the time to enjoy a lavish meal with friends.

Sour cream and dill

Many Russian dishes are served with sour cream and sprinkled liberally with dill. If you wish your dish to be garnish-free, say 'No sour cream' (без сметаны – *bez smetany*) or 'No dill' (без укропа – *bez ukropa*).

ZAKUSKI AND SALADS

The glory of the Russian table is the first course, the *zakuski* – salads, sliced smoked meats, smoked and salted fish, fresh and pickled vegetables, salted and

Solyanka

marinated mushrooms, and puff pastries (пирожки – *pirozhki*) filled with meat, potatoes, mushrooms, sautéed cabbage or fish. If you'd like a light meal, try a few of these starters.

Russian salads can be very complex (with inventive names and a long list of ingredients), or very simple, made traditionally of cucumbers and tomatoes (or radishes) seasoned with dill and with a sour cream or oil dressing. The classic mixed salad (винегрет – *vinegret*) is made of beetroot, potatoes, carrots and pickles, dressed with oil, mayonnaise or sour cream. Almost every restaurant has a version of the Salad 'Olivier' (салат «Оливье»), made of potatoes, onions, pickles and thin strips of meat (chicken, tongue or beef), and dressed with mayonnaise.

Russians eat a lot of fish – smoked, pickled, salted or baked with vegetables – as a starter. Herring (селёдка – *selyodka*) is traditionally served with fresh onions and boiled potatoes, or

Bliny with red caviar, sour cream and dill

buried under a rich salad of beetroot, potatoes, boiled egg and sour cream in the fancifully named 'herring under a fur coat' (селёдка под шубой – *selyodka pod shuboi*). You might also try fish in aspic (заливное из рыбы – *zalivnoe iz ryby*), usually served with horseradish.

Russian caviar comes from several kinds of sturgeon found in the Caspian Sea: the Beluga, Ossetra and Sevruga. A fourth kind of caviar comes from the sterlet, a young sturgeon that is now rare. This is imperial caviar and, should you find it (and can afford it), is golden yellow, with large, flavourful grains. Malossol, the delicate bluish-grey, lightly salted Beluga caviar, is one of the most highly prized for its slightly sweet and subtle flavour. Ossetra is light brown in colour and has a stronger fish taste. Sevruga has grey eggs and a robust flavour. Red salmon roe (красная икра – *krasnaya ikra*) has large red grains with a strong and salty flavour. All are eaten on bread or toast covered only with a bit of soft butter. Pancakes (блины – *bliny*) are served as a starter with caviar (икра – *ikra*).

Veal or beef in aspic (холодец – *kholodets*) is also served with horseradish as a starter, often with an assortment of smoked sausages (колбаса – *kolbasa*) and smoked meats (копченье – *kopchene*). For a hot starter, you could try a dish called Julienne (жюльен – *zhyulen*), a little pot of sliced mushrooms served in a white sauce topped with cheese and served bubbling hot from the oven.

SOUPS

Russians of the old school believe that a meal is not a meal without a bowl of soup. You can try borscht (борщ), a Ukrainian soup that Russians have adopted and annexed as their own. This beetroot soup can be made with fresh cabbage or sauerkraut, mushrooms, beef or even prunes. It is traditionally served with hot rolls called *pampushki* (пампушки), which are drizzled with garlic sauce. Another hearty soup is *pokhlyobki* (похлёбки), made from meat, poultry or fish with onions, potatoes and carrots, or *solyanka* (солянка), a slightly sour soup made of mushrooms, fish or meat seasoned with pickles, olives, capers and lemons and topped with sour cream.

☺ BEEF STROGANOV

Beef Stroganov was named after Count Alexander Stroganov, who was a governor general in the south of Russia and lived in Odessa. A wealthy and generous man who enjoyed the luxuries of life, he held 'open houses' where anyone who was well dressed and polite could stop in for lunch. For these luncheons, the count asked his chefs to invent a meat dish that could be easily served and eaten. The chefs came up with a dish that was something of a hybrid of French and Russian cuisine: tiny strips of beef served in a tomato and sour cream sauce. The dish was first popularised in Odessa cookbooks, where it was called Beef à la Stroganoff, and then was adapted throughout the empire – and eventually the world.

Lighter soups include mushroom (грибной – *gribnoy*), made with aromatic field mushrooms, most commonly porcini; a light fish soup (уха – *ukha*) seasoned with potatoes, carrots and onions; or clear chicken and noodle soups (куриная лапша – *kurinaya lapsha*). For good peasant fare, try cabbage soup (щи – *shchi*), made with fresh cabbage or sauerkraut, broth and seasoned with a dollop of sour cream.

In the summer, Russians enjoy *okroshka* (окрошка), an unusual gazpacho-style cold soup made of *kvas* (квас), a mildly alcoholic drink made from black bread, and diced vegetables, or a clear beetroot soup (свекольник – *svekolnik*) that is ladled over a salad of potatoes, cucumbers and radishes, dressed with sour cream and seasoned with dill or parsley.

MAIN DISHES

For a classic Russian main course, try *pelmeni* (пельмени), the Russian version of ravioli, made of a mixture of pork, beef and/or lamb wrapped in pasta dough. Upscale restaurants experiment with non-traditional fillings, like venison, rabbit or pumpkin.

For memories of imperial Russia, try Beef Stroganov in a rich sour cream sauce, or other pre-revolutionary dishes made of venison, boar, suckling pig, goose or duck, usually baked with apples or cabbage and served with a tart berry sauce. Russians are also proud of their cutlets (котлеты – *kotlety*), made of virtually any meat or combination, and fried until they are crisp on the outside, but succulent on the inside.

In most restaurants you order garnishes (гарнир – *garnir*) separately, from a choice that includes vegetables (овощи – *ovoshchi*), French fries (картофель фри – *kartofelfri*), mashed potatoes (картофельное пюре – *kartofelnoe pyure*) or buckwheat (гречневая каша – *grechnevaya kasha*).

DRINKS AND SWEETS

At the table, Russians drink mineral water, soda or a fruit drink: *mors* (морс), a refreshing drink made of fresh berries mixed with sugar and water, or juice (сок – *sok*). If you decide to try vodka with your starter, be sure to drink the Russian way: after a sip of vodka – or shot glass, depending on your stamina – immediately take a bite of food and a gulp of water or fruit drink. If you can't handle vodka, there are plenty of good Russian and imported wines to accompany your meals. Be sure to say whether you want dry (сухое – *sukhoe*) or sweet (сладкое – *sladkoe*). Russian sparkling wine (шампанское – *shampanskoe*) is also surprisingly good, although the best brut (брют) can be hard to find. You might also try some of the older pre-revolutionary drinks that are being revived, such as *sbiten'* (сбитень), a hot fermented drink made of honey and spices, and *medovukha* (медовуха), a spiced honey wine.

Meals end with tea (чай – *chay*), usually served with lemon, sugar and slices of cheese, or coffee (кофе – *kofe*), and a pastry (пирожное – *pirozhnoe*) or cake (торт – *tort*). You should also try Russian ice cream (мороженое – *morozhenoe*), which is deliciously rich and creamy, and usually served with berries or jam. A traditional sweet is *kisel* (кисель), a soft jelly made of fruits and thickened with cornflour.

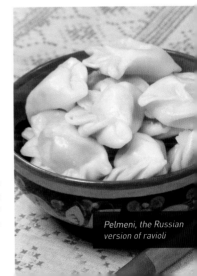

Pelmeni, the Russian version of ravioli

VEGETARIAN CUISINE

Most menus offer vegetarian pastas or grilled vegetables, and all the better restaurants provide a separate menu (постное меню – *postnoe menyu*) that includes no meat, fish or dairy products during the four religious fasts. During the rest of the year, tell the staff you are a vegetarian (вегетарианец – *vegetarianets*). There is usually an ample selection of salads and soups (овощной суп-пюре – *ovoshchnoy sup-pyure*), as well as potato-filled dumplings (вареники с картофелем – *vareniki s kartofelem*) and dozens of dishes made with mushrooms and grains. The cuisines from the Caucasus offer many vegetarian dishes, as do the Italian restaurants. Strict vegetarians should avoid clear soups that are more often than not made with chicken or beef stock.

TO HELP YOU ORDER...

Is there a table free? Есть свободный столик? **Est svobodny stolik?**

I'd like... Мне... **Mne...**

waiter/menu официант/меню **ofitsiant/menyu**

The bill, please Посчитайте, пожалуйста **Poschitayte, pozhaluysta**

bread хлеб **khleb**

butter масло **maslo**

coffee кофе **kofe**

dessert сладкое **sladkoe**

fish рыба **ryba**

fruit фрукты **frukti**

ice cream мороженое **morozhenoe**

meat мясо **myaso**

milk молоко **moloko**

pepper перец **perets**

potatoes картофель **kartofel**

rice рис **ris**

salad салат **salat**

salt соль **sol**

sandwich бутерброд **buterbrod**

soup суп **sup**

sugar сахар **sakhar**

wine вино **vino**

... AND READ THE MENU

porridge каша **kasha**

frankfurter сосиска **sosiska**

smoked/boiled sausage копчёная/варёная колбаса
  kopchyonaya/varyonaya kolbasa

pancake/bliny блины **bliny**

stuffed bliny блинчики **blinchiki**

potato salad салат «Столичный» **salat 'Stolichny'**

green salad зелёный салат **zelyony salat**

fresh vegetables свежие овощи **svezhie ovoshchi**

assorted fish/smoked meats рыбное/мясное ассорти
  rybnoe/myasnoe assorti

marinated mushrooms маринованные грибы
  marinovannye griby

beef/veal говядина/телятина **govyadina/telyatina**

pork свинина **svinina**

lamb баранина **baranina**

venison оленина **olenina**

chicken курица/цыплёнок **kuritsa/tsyplyonok**

duck утка **utka**

goose гусь **gus**

cod треска **treska**

trout форель **forel**

sturgeon осетрина **osetrina**

young sturgeon стерлядь **sterlyad**

crayfish раки **raki**

shrimp креветки **krevetki**

grilled на гриле **na grile**

fresh (pl) свежие **svezhie**

smoked (pl) копчёные **kopchyonye**

fried/sautéed (pl) жареные **zharenye**

baked/roasted (pl) тушёные **tushyonye**

PLACES TO EAT

We have used the following symbols to give an idea of the price of a three-course meal for two. The prices are a US dollar average, with drinks.

$$$$ over US$80
$$$ US$50–80
$$ US$30–50
$ under US$30

NEAR THE ADMIRALTY

1913 $$ *Ulitsa Dekabristov 2, tel: 812-315 5148*. This restaurant has the clean and simple interior of a neighbourhood bistro and offers good classic Russian cuisine from the year 1913; the last 'good' year in Russian history (before the start of World War I and the revolution). This is a great place to try Russian classics like 'herring under a fur coat', *solyanka* soup and handmade *pelmeni*. Good prices, large portions and friendly service.

Botanika $$ *Ulitsa Pestelya 7, tel: 812- 272 7091*, http://botanika.spb.ru. One of St Petersburg's top vegetarian hangouts, this friendly place serves meat-free Russian, Italian, Indian and Japanese dishes, all made using fresh ingredients. Culinary delights you thought you'd left behind when you boarded the plane to Russia, such as chutney, curry, muffins and Caesar salad, populate an imaginative and flavoursome menu.

Chaynaya Lozhka $ *Nevsky prospekt 44, tel: 812-571 4657*. The Teaspoon is a chain of Russian fast-food restaurants found across St Petersburg (and other Russian cities), serving up budget bliny, borsht, salads, lunch menus and sugary desserts. Great stop-off for lunch and it provides an interesting insight into what ordinary Russians really eat.

Kavkaz $$ *Karavannaya ulitsa 18, tel: 812-312 1665*, http://en.kavkaz-bar.ru. This no-nonsense restaurant serving quality Georgian food has been a favourite among locals for over a decade and a half.

Kilikia $$ *Nab. kanal Griboyedova 40, tel: 812-327 2208*. This unpretentious Armenian café has a simple exposed brick interior and is usually filled with members of the local Armenian community. The menu includes European dishes as well as excellent Armenian specialities, such as meat-filled dumplings and richly spiced stews.

La Russ $$$ *Nab. reki Moiki 37, tel: 812-571 7591*, www.laruss-spb.ru. La Russ recreates the atmosphere of the elegant *Orient Express*. Excellent traditional and modern Russian cuisine and six fun cabaret shows starting at 8.30pm.

Russian Empire $$$$ *Nevsky prospekt 17, tel: 812-571 2409* http://russianampir.ru. Is this the most elegant and expensive restaurant in Russia? In a restored section of the Stroganov Palace, sumptuous and rare French-influenced Russian cuisine is served on fine porcelain, with real silverware and Bohemian crystal.

Russian Vodka Room No 1 $$ *Konnogvardeysky bulvar 4, tel: 812-570 6420*, www.vodkaroom.ru. Attached to the Russian Vodka Museum, this restaurant serves dozens of traditional dishes from different historical periods. There's also 200 plus kinds of Russian vodka to choose from.

Troitsky Most $ *Nab. reki Moiki 30, tel: 812-925 5978*. There are several outlets of this vegetarian café around the city, all with the same cafeteria-style service as this one on the Petrograd Side. They offer about 10 salads (Russian and international), soups, mains and desserts. The portions are generous and the food is satisfying. A good place for vegetarians craving some tofu, or those wanting a break from Russian cuisine.

Tryufelny Dom Bruno $$$$ *Admiralteysky prospekt 10, tel: 812-940 1881*, http://dombruno.ru/en. Tryufelny Dom Bruno was established by acclaimed French chef Clement Bruno, 'the king of truffles'. Overlooking the Admiralty, it's one of the city's finest eating establishments (and the most expensive) – and the only one where truffles are added to each dish. Excellent service and atmosphere.

Vodograi $$ *Karavannaya ulitsa 2, tel: 812-570 5737*, http://vodograi.info. This Russian-themed restaurant, complete with costumed musicians and rural knick-knacks, plates up wholesome Russian specialities including borscht, *vareniki*, *pelmeni*, homemade sausages and rabbit in sour cream.

MID-NEVSKY PROSPEKT

Abrikosov Café $$ *Nevsky prospekt 40, tel: 812-312 2457*, www.abrikosov-spb.com. This exquisite café from 1906 still has the original Chinese silk wall panels and old signs asking the patrons not to smoke. It looks like a tourist trap, but it actually has good café food (like double-decker smoked salmon sandwiches) and sumptuous cakes and pastries, at prices that are surprisingly affordable.

Aragvi $$$ *Nab. reki Fontanki 9, tel: 812-570 5643*. The Aragvi provides a more elegant environment than other Georgian eateries normally do. The minimalist whitewashed walls, fireplace and simple wooden furniture are pleasantly clean and warm, and the food, from the garlic-laden salads to the succulent *shashlyk*, is very good.

Baku $$$ *Ulitsa Sadovaya 12/23, tel: 812-941 3756*. If you'd like to step into a sultan's palace, call in at this Azeri restaurant, with bright tiles, stained-glass windows and the warm colours of the south. The food is excellent, from rich salads to *plov* (pilaf) to *shashlyk*, especially the lamb.

Caviar Bar and Restaurant $$$$ *Mikhailovskaya ulitsa 1/7 (in the Grand Hotel Europe), tel: 812-329 6637*, www.belmond.com/grand-hotel-europe-st-petersburg. For a decadent splurge, spend an evening in the Caviar Bar of the Grand Hotel Europe, trying one – or more – of 35 kinds of vodka and one – or more – of 15 varieties of caviar. The restaurant also offers a business lunch and dinner menu featuring Russian and European classics.

Demidoff $$$$ *Nab. reki Fontanki 14, tel: 812-425 0147*. This upmarket restaurant with aristocratic 19th-century decor – including a working porcelain fireplace – is worth the expense. Demidoff serves traditional Russian haute cuisine with unusual twists, like salmon-stuffed *pelmeni* or duck roasted with honey, pine nuts, apples and fruit. Live music in the evenings.

Georgians $$ *Kolokolnaya ulitsa 8, tel: 812-315 9915*. A nice, small establishment in a quiet street close to the city centre. This value-for-money restaurant serves traditional Georgian dishes and Eastern European fare. The friendly staff help select the best Georgian wine to pair with the food.

Marius Pub $$ *Ulitsa Marata 11, tel: 812-315 4880*, http://mariuspub. ru. This pub attached to the Helvetia Hotel has a cosy bar and eating area and a pleasant terrace. Both are open 24 hours a day, providing an expat- and tourist-friendly assortment of higher-class pub grub and Russian fare.

Brasserie de Metropole $$ *Ulitsa Sadovaya 22, tel: 812-571 8888*. For generations, families have celebrated birthdays, graduations and other special occasions at this delightful café. The Metropole's cakes, pastries and confectionery are a delicious hybrid of French and Viennese sweets and St Petersburg creativity. A pleasant place to stop for a midday pick-me-up.

Palkin $$$$ *Nevsky prospekt 47, tel: 812-703 5371*, www.palkin.ru. The first Palkin tavern appeared in St Petersburg in 1785, and by the end of the 19th century there were several Palkin restaurants that were considered the finest eateries in the city. The last and best branch was closed in 1925, but in 2002, using photographs, archive material and advice from the Hermitage, Palkin opened once again at its former address. Despite the hype and prices, the decor is divine and the food is quite good, being a well-selected blend of pre-revolutionary aristocratic cuisine and French-influenced contemporary dishes.

Podval Brodyachey Sobaki (The Stray Dog Cellar) $$$ *Ploshchad Iskusstv 5/4, tel: 812-312 8047*. This basement café is a mecca for lovers of the Russian Silver Age. It was here that such luminaries as Osip Mandelstam and Anna Akhmatova read their poetry and sipped wine all through the night. Abandoned for decades, the site was slowly wheedled back from the city and opened once again as a café, art and performance centre. The walls are covered with exhibited art and there are performances (music, literary readings, jazz and folk music) every evening in one of the halls. The food is simple, ample and good Russian pub fare, some based on the original 1912 recipes.

Tolsty Fraer (Fat Friar) $$ *Dumskaya ulitsa 3, tel: 812-570 0102.* This chain of pubs has outlets all over the city, and although the decor is definitely student bar, the food is cheap and surprisingly good. They have their own brews, which should be enjoyed traditionally with either boiled crayfish or сухарики (*sukhariki*), decadent garlicky fried bread. But their mains, like the handmade cutlets, are also satisfying.

NEAR PLOSHCHAD VOSTANIYA

Chez Jules Café $$ *Ulitsa Gangutskaya 16, tel: 812-275 4953.* This tiny café near the Stieglitz Museum is French in ambience and multicultural in cuisine. It is a cosy and pleasant place with a fixed menu that blends European and Russian traditions in a simple fashion.

Bistrot Garçon $$$$ *Nevsky prospekt 95, tel: 812-717 2467.* The Bistrot Garçon is a cosy Parisian bistro dating from about 1945, with an antique ambience and chansons playing quietly in the background. The French chef prepares traditional and updated bistro fare, including terrines, fresh pastas and risottos, fanciful salads and such luxurious treats as warm foie gras with peaches and grilled veal.

Molokhovets' Dream $$$$ *Ulitsa Radishcheva 10, tel: 812-929 2247,* www.molokhovets.com. At the turn of the 20th century, Elena Molokhovets wrote her *Gift for Young Homemakers*, an enormous volume filled with recipes and advice for young wives. Now most of these recipes are outdated, but a fine Russian chef has transformed the best of them into one of St Petersburg's finest dining experiences. The small restaurant has understated decor, excellent service and very good, subtly updated aristocratic Russian cuisine accompanied by quiet live music.

Ukrop $$ *Ulitsa Marata 23, tel: 812-946 3036,* www.cafe-ukrop.ru. Pastas, salads and meat-free versions of Russian classics populate the refreshingly cheap menu of this vegetarian café-bistro. Portions are miserly.

TEATRALNAYA PLOSHCHAD AND KOLOMNA

Idiot $$ *Nab. reki Moiki 82, tel: 812-946 5173,* http://idiot-spb.com. The 'Idiot' is something of an expat legend: a warren of antique-filled and book-lined rooms serving vegetarian cuisine and lots of drinks (including a half-shot on the house just to get you going when you sit down).

Le'Chaim $$$ *Lermontovsky prospekt 2, tel: 812-572 5616,* https://spb-lehaim.ru. This kosher restaurant has elegant decor and delicious food that ranges from traditional (*latkes* and chicken schnitzel with mashed potatoes) to more adventurous (lightly pickled salmon with arugula and fried trout with roast potatoes, caraway seeds and rosemary).

Mansarda $$$$ *Pochtamskaya 3–5, tel: 812-640 1616.* This high-end Ginza Project restaurant at the Quattro Conti Business Center boasts breathtaking views of St Isaac's Cathedral. The delicious European and Russian food is equally stunning, although all this doesn't come cheap.

Mindal Cafe $$$ *Lermontovsky prospekt 30, tel: 812-714 6088,* http://mindalcafe.ru. This restaurant, opened in 2015, serves authentic Georgian and Russian fare, including excellent traditional game. Very convenient for post-performance dining near the Mariinsky Theatre. There are two further Mindal Cafe outlets in St Petersburg.

Teplo $$ *Bolshaya Morskaya ulitsa 45, tel: 812-570 1974,* www.v-teple.ru. One of St Petersburg's top dining spots, this cosy city-centre restaurant just off St Isaac's Square is a place most visitors find themselves returning to night after night. The experience is designed to give diners the feel they are eating in someone's house, creating a homely atmosphere in which you can slip off your shoes and relax after a hard day's sightseeing. The surprisingly affordable international menu features everything from Italian pastas to rack of lamb; the Napoleon cake comes highly recommended by the sweet-toothed groups and celebrities alike.

OUTSIDE THE CITY CENTRE

Chekhov $$$ *Petropavlovskaya 4, tel: 812-234 4511*, http://en.restaurant-chekhov.ru. Delicious Russian food is beautifully presented in a cosy atmosphere and stylish, old-fashioned surroundings. Beef Stroganov, chicken Kiev and home-made cordials are really worth a try here.

Pelmeni on Kronkverksky $$ *Kronverksky prospekt 55, tel: 812-415 4184*. This no-fuss restaurant offers a very wide selection of *pelmeni* and other traditional Russian fare. A convenient place for dining after visiting the zoo with children.

Russkaya Rybalka $$$ *Yuzhnaya doroga 11, tel: 812-416 0291*, http://russian-fishing-spb.ru. Located on an island where Prince Menshikov, Peter the Great's best friend, had his favourite fishing hole, you can fish in the pond and have the chef prepare your dish to order. As well as fun for kids, the food is quite good and elegant.

A-Z TRAVEL TIPS

A SUMMARY OF PRACTICAL INFORMATION

A

ACCOMMODATION

St Petersburg has a wide range of accommodation, from 'mini-hotels' – small private hotels made out of one or more renovated communal apartments – to Soviet-era monster hotels (now refurbished for the modern tourist) to some of the best five-star hotels in the world. Prices range from US$30 off season, in a modest mini-hotel, to stratospheric de luxe offerings. Another option is a serviced apartment, which includes registration, maid service and usually cable TV and either Wi-fi or high-speed internet. They can be found on www.waytorussia.net, or through private firms, such as www.nevskyinn.ru or www.nevsky88.com.

Booking well ahead is only really necessary around New Year and in early May when many Russians take a long break around two national holidays.

> I'd like a single/double room **Мне, пожалуйста, одноместный/двухместный номер.** Mne, pozhaluysta, odnomestny/dvukhmestny nomer.
> What's the rate per night? **Сколько стоит номер за одни сутки?** Skolko stoit nomer za odni sutki?
> My lamp/television doesn't work. **Лампа/телевизор не работает.** Lampa/televizor ne rabotaet.

AIRPORTS

Pulkovo (LED; www.pulkovoairport.ru). This is the main airport in St Petersburg and is located about 17km (11 miles) south of the city. It is divided into **Pulkovo 1** (domestic flights and flights to the former Soviet republics) and **Pulkovo 2**, which is around ten minutes' away and handles international flights.

For first-time visitors, it is best to use the airport transfer services provided by your hotel (about US$40) or one of the official taxis (about US$60) ordered from a booth in the arrivals hall. Under no circumstances should you use the services of the unofficial taxi drivers who approach you in the terminal. If you feel adventurous and don't have much baggage, you can take Bus 39 or 39A (from Pulkovo 2) to Moskovskaya metro station, or one of the many mini-buses K39 (маршрутное такси – *marshrutnoe taksi*) to the city centre.

B

BUDGETING FOR YOUR TRIP

As elsewhere in Russia, St Petersburg can be eye-wateringly expensive one minute and surprisingly good value for money the next. Be aware that during White Nights prices go up by about 30 percent.

Flights. Expect to pay around £300 for a direct return flight from London to St Petersburg when booked well in advance, perhaps slightly less if you are willing to change planes somewhere on the Continent (such as Rome or Kyiv).

Accommodation. For a budget double room per night, expect to pay up to US$100, mid-range US$100–200, high-end US$200–300 and for de luxe over US$300.

Meals. A three-course dinner for two, with drinks, can be had in one of the many modest restaurants and cafés for US$30 or less. Expect to pay significantly more in elegant restaurants.

Museums. Two-tiered pricing system with higher entrance for foreigners, at around US$11–12, operates in many of the city's museums. Entry to the main building of the Hermitage and its other buildings costs about US$12.

Entertainment. If you don't opt for the best box seats, theatre and concert tickets are US$10–20, and opera and ballet up to US$50.

Transport. Taxis around the city are usually under US$10, even through car services. A car and driver cost US$15–100 an hour (depending on the class of car), but one ride on the metro (regardless of distance) costs around US$1.

C

CLIMATE

St Petersburg's climate is tempered by the proximity of the sea, so although the temperatures might be higher than inland cities at the same latitude, the damp makes it feel much colder. Spring arrives in April or May, summers are warm but rarely scorching hot, by late August temperatures become autumnal, and the first snow can fall in October or November. December until March is usually cold and snowy. In the height of the summer White Nights, the sun virtually never sets – but in the depth of winter there are only about six hours of pallid light.

	J	F	M	A	M	J	J	A	S	O	N	D
min												
°C	-8	-8	-5	1	7	12	14	13	8	4	-2	-6
°F	18	18	24	34	44	53	58	55	47	39	28	22
max												
°C	-4	-4	2	9	15	20	22	20	14	8	1	-2
°F	25	25	36	48	60	68	72	68	58	47	34	28

CLOTHING

Young and wealthy Russians are very fashion-conscious, but average residents are not. You will rarely need formal dress; people attend the opera straight from work, so unless you want to dress up, you don't need to. In the summer, be sure to bring a sweater and rainwear (including waterproof shoes). In winter, you will need to bring a heavy coat or down jacket, hat, gloves, scarf and boots that grip snow and ice.

Buildings, however, tend to be overheated, so you are unlikely to need heavy sweaters inside. Almost all museums, restaurants and businesses insist that you leave outerwear in the cloakroom (гардероб – *garderob*) as soon as you enter the building (tipping not required).

The city streets are rarely well cleaned, which means they are coated with a thick layer of ice in the winter and an equally thick layer of mud at all other times of the year. Be sure to bring comfortable low-heeled shoes or boots that can withstand ice, mud, slush and puddles.

CRIME AND SAFETY

St Petersburg is probably safer than most major European cities. You should take the normal precautions for any large city: put valuables in the hotel safe, don't carry large amounts of cash and beware of pickpockets in crowded places (including the metro) or markets. Avoid the parks at night and don't drink with 'new friends' anywhere, and particularly not at the railway station. Change money in marked change booths only, and be sure to count the cash that you take from the sliding drawer (there is a scam in which one banknote gets stuck in the drawer thanks to a bit of glue). Do not fall for another scam in which a large wad of bills is 'dropped' in the street; if you pick it up, the person who 'dropped it' will return and insist the sum was twice what you picked up.

Nationalism and racism in Russia has become a serious problem, escalated by increases in anti-immigration sentiment since the global financial crisis in 2008. Skinheads (recognisable by their shaved

I've been robbed. **Меня ограбили.** Menya ograbili.
My passport/visa was stolen. **Украли мой паспорт/мою визу.** Ukrali moy pasport/moyu vizu.
I want to file a complaint with the police. **Я хочу написать заявление в полицию.** Ya khochu napisat zayavlenie v politsiyu.
I need a document from the police about the crime for my insurance. **Чтобы получить страховку, мне нужна справка из полиции.** Chtoby poluchit strakhovku, mne nuzhna spravka iz politsii.

heads, black or military-style clothing) prey on blacks, Asians and dark-skinned people. Avoid groups of them, particularly at night on the metro.

If you are robbed, you will need to go to the police station to file a report and get a *spravka*, an official document registering the crime, which you'll need for the insurance settlement. Your hotel or the tourist information office (see page 131) can assist you.

D

DISABLED TRAVELLERS

St Petersburg is not a disabled-person friendly city. Some of the Western-run and owned hotels, like the Petro Palace, Radisson Blu and Kempinski, have wheelchair-accessible rooms and public spaces. A few of the main museums, like the Hermitage, are barrier-free. Since tourists in wheelchairs will need to be carried upstairs, it is recommended to bring a lighter manual chair.

E

ELECTRICITY

Russia has 220V/50Hz AC, with European-style round two-pin sockets. However, some older Russian sockets are narrower than European standard pins; ask the concierge or reception desk for an adaptor (переходник – *perekhodnik*).

EMBASSIES AND CONSULATES

Australia: Petrovsky prospekt 14, tel: 812-325 7334
Canada: Starokonyushenny Pereulok 23, Moscow, tel: 0495-925 6000
Ireland: Grokholsky Pereulok 5, Moscow, tel: 0495-937 5911
New Zealand: Ulitsa Povarskaya 44, Moscow, tel: 0495-956 3579
South Africa: Granatny Pereulok 1, Building 9, Moscow, tel: 0495-926 1177

UK: Ploshchad Proletarskoy diktatury 5, tel: 812-320 3200
US: Furshtatskaya ulitsa 15, tel: 812-331 2600

> Where is the US/UK embassy? **Где американское/британское консольство?** Gde amerikanskoe/britanskoe konsolstvo?
> I want to speak with my consul. **Я хочу поговорить с моим консулом.** Ya khochu pogovorit s moim konsulom.

EMERGENCIES

Russia uses the standard European emergency number, **112**. The four old emergency numbers are, however, still in use. Operators normally only speak Russian:

Fire **01**

Police **02**

Ambulance **03**

Gas **04**

Russians are very responsive to someone in need, be it a minor problem (getting lost, breaking a shoe) or a major emergency (being robbed, becoming ill). If you are in trouble, walk up to someone and start talking; the person will try to find an English speaker or help.

> Help! **Помогите!** Pomogite!
> Police! **Полиция!** Politsiya!
> Call an ambulance! **Позвоните в скорую помощь!** Pozvonite v skoruyu pomoshch!
> I'm/we're lost! **Я/мы заблудил(ся)/(ась)/(ись)!** Ya/my zabludilsya/zabludilas/zabludilis (masculine singular/feminine singular/plural)

G

GETTING THERE (See also Airports)

By air. Although there are flights daily from nearly 40 European cities, passengers from North America, Australia and New Zealand will have a stopover.

By ship. Ferries arrive from Sweden, Germany, Finland and Estonia. Most trips take about 14 hours overnight.

By rail. Trains from the Baltic and Eastern European countries take between 15 and 37 hours. Be aware that you will need a transit visa, obtained in advance, to pass through Belarus. Trains from the west arrive at Vitebsky Station. Three trains leave Helsinki every day; they take from about six to eight hours and arrive at Ladozhsky Station. From the east, trains from Beijing and Vladivostok make the week-long trip several times a week.

GUIDES AND TOURS

Many companies provide package tours to St Petersburg that include visa, hotel, meals and tours. For independent travellers, city tours and a variety of suburban palace tours are run every day in English by the trustworthy and competent Eclectica-Guide. Their kiosk is at the southeast corner of Gostiny Dvor (tel: 812-610 0540; www.eclectica-guide. ru). They can also arrange individual tours.

Peter's Walking Tours run interesting tours of the city, including

We'd like an English-speaking guide/an English interpreter. **Нам нужен англоязычный экскурсовод/ переводчик.** Nam nuzhen angloyazychny ekskursovod/ perevodchik.

Do you have tours in English? **У вас есть экскурсия на английском?** U vas est ekskursiya na angliyskom?

a bicycle tour on Saturday and Sunday over the summer. For most of them, you just turn up at the meeting point a few minutes before the tour starts. A list of tours can be found at www.peterswalk.com.

Another option is a freelance guide. Check the forums at www.expat. ru, www.redtape.ru or www.waytorussia.net. They charge about US$15/hour and can often provide a car and driver at extra cost. Some museums have English-speaking guides; book in advance.

H

HEALTH AND MEDICAL CARE

No vaccinations are compulsory for St Petersburg and Russia, and the only city-specific health risk is the tap water, which you should not drink. Inexpensive mineral water (минеральная вода – *mineralnaya voda*) is available virtually everywhere.

Bring all necessary prescription drugs and have medical insurance that covers you abroad and includes medical evacuation. Russian health care is underfinanced and patchy; in case of illness, seek help at a clinic catering to foreigners. Bring insurance forms with you; in most cases you will have to pay for the services and be reimbursed when

Where's the nearest (all-night) pharmacy? **Где ближайшая (круглосуточная) аптека?** Gde blizhayshaya (kruglosutochnaya) apteka?

I need a doctor/dentist. **Мне нужен врач/зубной врач.** Mne nuzhen vrach/zubnoy vrach.

an ambulance **скорая помощь** skoraya pomoshch

a hospital **больница** bolnitsa

I have a stomach/toothache. **У меня болит желудок/зуб** U menya bolit zheludok/zub.

I have a fever. **У меня температура.** U menya temperatura.

you return home. Two clinics that provide 24/7 services, with English-speaking and trained physicians, including dentistry, are:

American Medical Clinic, Nab. reki Moiki 78, tel: 812-740 2090, www.amclinic.com.

MEDEM International Clinic and Hospital, Ulitsa Marata 6, tel: 812-336 3333, www.medem.ru.

Pharmacies (аптека – apteka) are much more common than in the West – look for them within large stores and at metro stations. Most are open 8am–8pm. There are all-night pharmacies in every district; look for the number '24' or ask at your hotel. 36.6 is a good Western-style pharmacy chain.

L

LANGUAGE

St Petersburg is trying to become more tourist-friendly, with signs, museum notes and even menus in English, but basic familiarity with the Cyrillic alphabet is strongly recommended.

In this guide, we have used the simplified system of transliteration provided below. Note that many male Russian names and adjectives end in -ой, -ий or -ый, which we transliterate as 'y'. In some cases, letters are transliterated as pronounced, such as the endings -oro, -ero (-evo, -ovo), and some names, like Tchaikovsky or Gorbachev, are given in the form that has become standard in English. Don't worry about soft and hard sounds; if you can hit most of the consonants in a word, people will understand you.

Russian / Transliteration / English Example

А а / a / a in father
Б б / b / b in book
В в / v / v in very
Г г / g / g in good
Д д / d / d in day
Е е / e (ye when first letter in a word) / ye in yet (note that words like

Hello **Здравствуйте** Zdravstvuyte
Good morning **Доброе утро** Dobroe utro
Good day/evening **Добрый день/вечер** Dobry den/vecher
Goodbye **До свидания** Do svidaniya
Please **Пожалуйста** Pozhaluysta
Thank you **Спасибо** Spasibo
Help! **Помогите!** Pomogite!
Good/bad **Хорошо/плохо** Khorosho/plokho
I don't speak Russian **Я не говорю по-русски** Ya ne
    govoryu po-russki
I don't understand **Я не понимаю** Ya ne ponimayu
Toilet W/M **Туалет Ж/М** Tualet Zh/M
Danger **Опасно** Opasno
Open/closed **Открыто/закрыто** Otkryto/zakryto
Where/when/how/who/why **Где/когда/как/кто/почему**
    Gde/kogda/kak/kto/pochemu
Start/continuation of exhibition **Начало/продолжение
    осмотра** Nachalo/prodolzhenie osmotra
Shoe covers **Бахилы** Bakhili
Entrance/exit **Вход/выход** Vkhod/vykhod
Cashier/ticket office **Касса** Kassa

'lobnoe' are pronounced lob-noi-ye)
Ё ё / yo / yo in yonder
Ж ж / zh / s in pleasure or composure
З з / z / z in zoo
И и / i / ee in meet
Й й / y / y in boy
К к / k / k in kite
Л л / l / l in lamp
М м / m / m in map

Н н / n / n in not
О о / o / o in pot
П п / p / p in pet
Р р / r / r in restaurant (rolled r)
С с / s / s in sound
Т т / t / t in tip
У у / u / oo in hoot
Ф ф / f / f in face
Х х / kh / ch in Channukah (a guttural kh)
Ц ц / ts / ts in sits
Ч ч / ch / ch in chip
Ш ш / sh / sh in shut
Щ щ / shch / shch in fresh cheese
Ъ ъ / / Placed after a consonant, this keeps the sound hard
Ы ы / y / i in ill
Ь ь / / Placed after a consonant, this makes the sound palletised (soft)
Э э / e / e in extra
Ю ю / yu / u in use
Я я / ya / ya in yard

LGBTQ TRAVEL

Homosexuality was a crime in Soviet times and is still condemned by the Russian Orthodox Church and many Russians old and young. Skinheads and religious groups have targeted some gay clubs in St Petersburg and have attacked clients when they leave. The police are sometimes indifferent (or worse) to complaints from the LGBTQ community and laws concerning the promotion of homosexuality in public have not helped the situation. However, despite the church and state's stance, attitudes have shifted slightly over the last decade among the general public, and St Petersburg even has a gay club scene. The site www.gay.ru has an extensive English-language section with listings for bars, clubs, guides and other entertainment. For more information, contact Together at together@gay.ru.

M

MAPS

Good maps in Russian and English are available at tourist centres (see page 131), in bookshops, in many museums and in virtually all hotels.

MEDIA

Most hotels provide cable television with a full array of English-language news and entertainment channels. Newsstands in major hotels as well as foreign-owned supermarkets have current English-language magazines and the *International Herald Tribune*.

The glossy monthly *Pulse St Petersburg* provides feature stories and cultural listings, as does *Where*, which can be found in hotels and many restaurants. Several other official and unofficial (i.e. commercial) guides can be found around the city. They are published quarterly, with cultural listings and feature articles.

MONEY

The currency in Russia is the rouble, which consists of 100 kopeks. There are bills in denominations of 10 (being phased out), 50, 100, 500, 1,000 and 5,000, and coins of one, five, 10 and 50 kopeks, as well as one, two, five and 10 roubles.

Cash machines/ATMs (банкомат – *bankomat*) can be found throughout the city and are considered secure these days, although be sure to take the usual safety precautions at street terminals.

I'd like to exchange money. **Я хочу обменять деньги.** Ya khochu obmenyat dengi.

Do you accept credit cards? **Вы принимаете кредитные карты?** Vy prinimaete kreditnye karty?

Exchange offices (обмен – *obmen*). Only exchange money at official exchange offices, in banks or hotels. Only pristine notes will be accepted (no tears, stains, writing) and expect much scrutiny and partial rejection of the currency you present to cashiers. Dollars and euros are the best currencies to bring; British pounds can be more difficult to exchange.

O

OPENING TIMES

There are no reliable standard opening and closing times. Banks and state offices open their doors at about 8.30am and close at 6 or 7pm, often with an hour off for lunch. Most shops open around 10 or 11am and close at 8 to 10pm; a few still close for lunch. Restaurants often stay open until the last client has left, and there are hundreds of 24-hour kiosks, food shops, cafés and clubs. Each museum has its own idiosyncratic hours.

P

POLICE

Rebranded to appear cuddlier and friendlier, the Russian police (полиция – *politsiya*) still stop locals and tourists for document checks. Hand them your documents but not your purse or wallet (money has been known to disappear during checks). Despite their patchy reputation, most officers try their best to be helpful and kind if you are lost or in trouble, though few speak English. Your hotel or

Where's the nearest police station? **Где ближайшее отделение полиции?** Gde blizhayshee otdelenie politsii?

the tourist centre (see page 131) can provide assistance should it be required.

Main Police Station Suvorovsky prospect 50/52 (nearest metro station Ploshchad Vostanniya), tel: 812-573 2676.

POST OFFICES

The Russian postal system (почта – *pochta*) is still slow, though most letters, parcels and postcards eventually reach their destination. Cards and letters can usually be posted from your hotel. Express service should be handled by one of the international courier companies operating in the city: DHL (www.dhl.ru) or TNT Express (www.tnt.com).

PUBLIC HOLIDAYS

Russian state holidays are:

1–7 January New Year and Orthodox Christmas
23 February Defenders of the Homeland Day
8 March International Women's Day
1 May Spring and Labour Holiday
9 May Victory Day
12 June Russia Day
4 November People's Unity Day

When holidays fall on Tuesday or Thursday, Monday or Friday are usually days off, with the Saturday after the holiday a working day. Embassies are closed on Russian and national holidays.

R

RELIGION

When entering Orthodox churches, women must cover their heads and men must remove hats and caps. Shorts and skirts are frowned upon. Never touch the icons and you may need permission to photograph inside a place of worship.

T

TELEPHONES

The country code for Russia is 7 and the city code for St Petersburg is 812. For local calls, public telephones can be found near and in metro stations. You can buy a phonecard (телефонная карта – *telefonnaya karta*) at a ticket office in denominations of 20 and 50 minutes.

To make an international call, dial 8 and wait for the dial tone to repeat, then 10, then the country and city codes and number.

International telephone fees in hotels are exorbitant, and it is much cheaper to buy a calling card (also called телефонная карта) from one of the mobile-phone centres or booths near every major intersection and metro station.

TIME ZONES

St Petersburg is GMT plus three hours. In 2014, Russia ceased observing the Daylight Saving Time and switched to permanent standard time.

TIPPING

Tipping is rather haphazard; expected but not mandatory. In restaurants, cafés and bars, rounding up the bill is sufficient. Taxi drivers and hotel staff expect tips for assisting with bags (20–50 roubles) and tour guides will also welcome a tip (200 roubles or more, if the service was good).

TOILETS

There are paid public toilets (usually blue plastic) by metro stations and in most public parks; public toilets can also be found in every mall and museum. Facilities in restaurants, cafés and bars are gen-

Where is the toilet? **Где здесь туалет?** Gde zdes tualet?

erally clean, but they may not always have toilet paper.

TOURIST INFORMATION

The tourist information service (http://eng.ispb.info) runs tourist centres on Palace Square (Dvortsovaya ploshchad 12) and at Ulitsa Sadovaya 37, as well as several other locations around the city centre, including the airport. These provide free maps, assistance and advice and are generally open 10am–7pm. Area maps can be found on stands outside most metro stations.

TRANSPORT

St Petersburg has an excellent and cheap public transport system. With traffic worsening, the fastest way to get anywhere is underground.

Metro. The stations are marked with a red 'M'. Inside the station, buy tokens at the ticket office (or through machines), pop one into the turnstile and hop on the fast-moving escalator. Services run from around 6am until midnight.

Where can I get a taxi? **Где можно найти такси?** Gde mozhno nayti taksi?

What's the fare to...? **Сколько стоит проезд до...?** Skolko stoit proezd do...?

Where is the nearest bus stop/metro station? **Где ближайшая остановка автобуса/станция метро?** Gde blizhaishaya ostanovka avtobusa/stantsiya metro?

Will you tell me when to get off? **Вы подскажете, когда мне выходить?** Vy podskazhete, kogda mne vykhodit?

What's the next stop/station? **Какая следующая остановка/станция?** Kakaya sleduyushchaya ostanovka/stantsiya?

Trams, trolleybuses and buses. Hop on and pay the fare to the conductor, who somehow manages to make the rounds between stops. In mini-buses (маршрутки – marshrutki), you pay the driver directly. **Taxis.** You will find these clustered around hotels and a few main squares. It is difficult to catch a cab cruising the streets. However, if you stand on the road and hold your hand out, in a few minutes 'private cab drivers' (i.e. people moonlighting in their own cars) will undoubtedly stop. Despite the apparent danger, this is the standard way to get around the city. The main safety precautions are to avoid any car with one or more additional passengers and to get a cab with a trusted friend in tow, if possible. State your destination and your price (usually around 200 roubles for a short distance, up to 500 or more for a long distance or at night) and hop in.

V

VISAS AND ENTRY REQUIREMENTS

All visitors to Russia must have a visa and a passport valid for six months after departure, with at least two free pages for the visa and stamps. There are three ways you can obtain a visa:

Arrange your trip through an agency as part of a group or individual tour – the agency will handle all the visa formalities for you.

Arrange a tourist visa yourself – this means you will have to book the hotel and return ticket before applying. Full instructions, addresses and fees are listed on Russian embassy sites in each country. Tourist visas are issued for up to one month and cannot be extended.

Apply through an agency such as Real Russia (www.realrussia. co.uk) who will do all the legwork for you for a fee.

When you arrive in the country, you must fill in a migration card. Airlines provide them onboard, and attendants help you fill them out. You must be registered during your stay. This is arranged by hotels or the inviting agency (including visa and tour companies and most apartment rental agencies). A receipt proves legal registration.

W

WEBSITES AND INTERNET ACCESS

The vast majority of hotels and hostels provide free or paid Wi-fi for their guests. Rare is the restaurant or café in Russia that doesn't have Wi-fi access for those who eat and drink there. Internet cafés are virtually a thing of the past, though there are a few free Wi-fi hotspots (in Peterhof Park for instance). The country's website suffix is .ru.

Some useful addresses are:

www.petersburgcity.com Full listings service in English
www.gotorussia.com Russia travel website
www.redtape.ru Expat and tourist forum and information
www.expat.ru Expat website with lots of advice for travellers
www.restoran.ru/spb Restaurant listings and a reservation service
http://eng.ispb.info Official tourist board website
www.saint-petersburg.com Unofficial tourism website

Y

YOUTH HOSTELS

Theatre Hostel Nekrasova ulitsa 12, tel: 812-272 5401, www.hostel-puppet.ru. Dorm bed US$15–20.

Nord Hostel Ulitsa Bolshaya Morskaya 10, tel: 812-571 0342, www.nord hostel.com. Dorm bed US$32.

Baby Lemonade Hostel Ulitsa Inzhenernaya 7, tel: 812-570 7943, http://epoquehostels.com. Dorm bed US$15–22.

Friends Life Nevsky Prospekt 47, tel: 812-331 7799, www.en.friendsplace.ru. Dorm bed US$24–30.

Location Hostel Ligovsky Prospekt 74, tel: 812-329 1274, www.location-hostel.ru. Dorm bed US$18.

RECOMMENDED HOTELS

Hotel prices are usually listed in roubles, sometimes in currency 'units' (dollars or euros), which the hotel itself defines. Be sure to enquire about the hotel exchange rate so you know the cost in your currency, and clarify whether the quoted price includes the 18 percent VAT.

The hotels listed are located in the city centre and provide visa support, free Wi-fi, cable TV and breakfast, unless otherwise noted.

As a basic guide we have used the symbols below to indicate the price per night for a double room with bath. Note that prices rise about 20–30 percent during the peak season of White Nights.

$$$$	over US$300
$$$	US$200–300
$$	US$100–200
$	under US$100

NEAR THE ADMIRALTY AND HERMITAGE

Angleterre Hotel $$$$ *Ulitsa Malaya Morskaya 24, tel: 812-494 5666,* www.angleterrehotel.com. Completely renovated, this elegant hotel is an oasis of luxury and comfort. Located across from St Isaac's Cathedral, next to its sister hotel the Astoria, it has 192 rooms and suites, a well-equipped fitness centre with sauna and small pool and several celebrated restaurants. Breakfast not included.

Astoria $$$$ *Ulitsa Bolshaya Morskaya 39, tel: 812-494 5757,* www.rocco fortehotels.com. The Astoria is one of the city's grand old hotels, built in 1912 and now fully renovated. The hotel has 169 rooms and suites, and every service anyone could wish for, including a full spa and 24-hour fitness centre, parquet floors, linen curtains and marble bathrooms. A truly sumptuous hotel, right in the city centre.

Central Inn – Atmosphera $$ *Ulitsa Yakubovicha 2, tel: 812-921 1540,* http://a-hotel.spb.ru. This mini-hotel is right next to St Isaac's Cathedral, with 15 modern rooms, gym, sauna and pleasant café. It is rather modest, but the staff are extremely helpful and friendly. Visa support arranged through an affiliate agency.

Comfort Hotel $$ *Ulitsa Bolshaya Morskaya 25, tel: 812-570 6700,* www. comfort-hotel.ru. Located in the same building as the Herzen House, Comfort Hotel is accessible by lift, with 18 modern rooms and all the amenities you might expect.

Fortecia Piter $$ *Ulitsa Millionaya 29, tel: 812-315 0828.* Literally steps from the Hermitage, this courtyard mini-hotel puts you right in the heart of the action. The eight rooms are on the cramped side but furnished with modern fabrics.

Herzen House $$ *Ulitsa Bolshaya Morskaya 25, tel: 812-571 5098,* www. herzen-hotel.com. This commendable mini-hotel is accessed by a lift and has 29 modern rooms with high ceilings and a full range of amenities. It is located a few blocks from the Hermitage in an area with plenty of restaurants and cafés.

Kempinski Hotel Moika 22 $$$$ *Nab. reki Moiki 22, tel: 812-335 9111,* www.kempinski.com. The Kempinski has refurbished several old mansions into a luxurious hotel, with a spacious atrium, cosy wood-lined bar (with fireplace), wine-cellar bar and tea-room (with fireplace and live classical music). There are nearly 200 rooms, a fitness centre and a terrific café, the Bellevue Brasserie on the top floor, with a fabulous 360-degree view of the city centre.

Moyka 5 $$ *Nab. reki Moiki 5, tel: 812-601 0636,* www.moyka5hotel.com. Moyka 5 is a bright little yellow house with 24 modern rooms of various classes (including split-level apartments with Jacuzzis and great views of the city). The public spaces have antique decor and there is a cheerful breakfast room.

Nevsky Inn 1 and 2 $ *Kirpichny pereulok 2, Apt 19, tel: 812-972 6873* and *Malaya Morskaya 9, Apt 3, tel: 812-312 2686,* www.nevskyinn.ru. These small bed-and-breakfast inns (with seven and four rooms respectively) are comfortable and cheap, with some of the most friendly service in town. The Kirpichny pereulok address is a fourth-floor 'walk-up'; the smaller Inn is on the second floor. Both are located within two blocks of the Hermitage.

Old Vienna $$ *Ulitsa Malaya Morskaya 13 (entrance on Gorokhovaya ulitsa), tel: 812-312 9339,* www.old-spb.ru. Part of the Bygone Petersburg mini-hotel chain, this boutique hotel was once one of St Petersburg's most famous bohemian cafés at the turn of the 20th century. The fawn-green halls and rotunda café-breakfast room (where photos show St Petersburg's famous writers and artists dining just before the revolution) are decorated in Art Nouveau style. Each of the 14 rooms is dedicated to an artist or writer of the Silver Age. No visa support.

Petro Palace Hotel $$$$ *Ulitsa Malaya Morskaya 14, tel: 812-571 3006,* www.petropalacehotel.com. The Petro Palace was once the mansion of Baron von Stahl and is now a rather elegant medium-sized hotel, fully renovated in 2013, serving both business clients and tourists. The public spaces are filled with columns, marble and antiques, while the rooms boast standard classical decor. The hotel has a large fitness centre, including pool and sauna. Breakfast not included with most rates.

Pushka Inn $$ *Nab. reki Moiki 14, tel: 812-644 7120,* www.pushka-inn.com. Pushka Inn is located in a superbly refurbished 18th-century house, with public spaces that retain the building's original features and rooms that are simple and modern. A very cosy and inviting boutique hotel with 33 rooms, overlooking the Moika river in the city centre.

Renaissance Baltic $$$$ *Pochtamtskaya ulitsa 4, tel: 812-380 4000,* http://renaissance-hotels.marriott.com. This top-class contemporary hotel is three blocks from Nevsky prospekt, with a great deal of charm, from the airy atrium to the comfortable rooms, fitness centre, bars and restaurants. This is an upmarket hotel with a more personal touch.

Residence on Gorokhovaya $ *Gorokhovaya ulitsa 8, tel: 812-312 7377,* www.residencehotels.ru. This tiny, four-room mini-hotel is a 'walk-up' through rather run-down hallways, but its friendly staff, central location, modern rooms and excellent prices make it a great deal.

W Hotel $$$$ *Voznesensky prospekt 6, tel: 812-610 6161,* www.wstpeters-burg.com. From the retro-styled lobby to the 137 minimalist rooms that make guests feel as if they've stepped onto a 1960s Bond movie set, this hotel is something special in a special city. Forget elegant palaces and Art Nouveau, this is the 21st century, with all the mod cons that go with it.

MID-NEVSKY PROSPEKT

Antique Hotel Rachmaninov $$ *Kazanskaya ulitsa 5, tel: 812-571 9778,* www.hotelrachmaninov.com. Although this hotel is a third-floor 'walk-up', the stunning location (a few steps from Nevsky) and charming interior make the walk worthwhile. The halls are whitewashed brick, the rooms have pine furniture and wooden floors and there is a bright lounge filled with antique furniture. The Rachmaninov Suite, where the composer lived as a child, has a tiny balcony with a fabulous view of the Kazan Cathedral and Nevsky prospekt.

Hotel Baskof $$ *pereulok Baskov 6, tel: 812-272 6493,* www.baskof-hotel.com. This eight-room mini-hotel has updated Silver Age decor (including a white ceramic corner stove in one of the rooms) with comfortable rooms and a full range of modern facilities. It is tucked away on a quiet street not far from the Fontanka and Nevsky prospekt.

Corinthia Nevskij Palace Hotel $$$$ *Nevsky prospekt 57, tel: 812-380 2001,* www.corinthia.com. This old hotel provides traditional Western-standard comfort and services in a 19th-century palace right on Nevsky prospekt. It has a good-sized fitness centre and a fine choice of cafés and restaurants. Breakfast not included.

Dostoevsky $$$ *Vladimirsky prospekt 19, tel: 812-331 3200,* www.dostoevsky-hotel.com. The Dostoevsky occupies the top floors of the *style moderne* Vladimirsky Passazh arcade, with restaurants and shops nearby, as well as a fitness centre and sauna. The public spaces have old-world, elegant decor, but its 200-plus rooms are very modern.

Grand Hotel Europe $$$$ *Mikhailovskaya ulitsa 1/7, tel: 812-329 6000,* www.grandhoteleurope.com. Over 140 years old, this is one of the world's best hotels with a guest list to prove it. In recent years the Grand Hotel Europe has welcomed a pantheon of stars, from Queen Elizabeth and Bill Clinton to Sting and Jane Fonda. In the old days it was the hotel of choice for Lord and Lady Astor, not to mention Pyotr Tchaikovsky, George Bernard Shaw and Grigory Rasputin. Beautiful rooms, impeccable service, five restaurants, fitness and business centres, but rather bizzarely breakfast is not included.

Helvetia Hotel & Suites $$$ *Ulitsa Marata 11, tel: 812-326 5353,* https://helvetiahotel.ru. The Helvetia seems more like a friendly apartment building than a hotel, with guest entrances accessed through an open courtyard filled with flowers in the summertime. This stylishly refurbished mansion has studio and family suites with kitchens, making it one of the best places in the city for families to bed down.

Radisson Royal $$$$ *Nevsky prospekt 49/2, tel: 812-322 5000,* www.radissonblu.com. The people at Radisson gutted a building dating from the 1730s, saving the facade but constructing a first-rate, up-to-the-minute hotel inside. As you would expect, it provides a high standard of service and amenities, including a fitness centre, slap bang in the midst of the city-centre action.

Hotel Vesta $$ *Nevsky prospekt 90–92, tel: 812-272 0544,* www.vesta-hotel.ru. Even though this hotel's address is on roaring Nevsky prospekt, it is actually tucked away from the crowds in a pleasant courtyard. The rooms are all modern European style and standard, although a few period features from centuries past have survived in the public rooms. The hotel caters to both tourists and business travellers.

NEAR PLOSHCHAD VOSTANIYA

Hotel Brothers Karamazov $$ *Ulitsa Sotsialisticheskaya 11-A, tel: 812-335 1185,* www.karamazovhotel.com. The Brothers Karamazov Hotel is located in the heart of Dostoevsky territory, about a 20-minute walk from Nevsky prospekt. The small hotel (28 rooms) has clean classical decor with some antiques in the public spaces and larger rooms. It caters to both tourists and business travellers, and has a restaurant that serves a well-selected range of traditional Russian and European dishes.

Grand Hotel Emerald $$$$ *Suvorovsky prospekt 18, tel: 812-740 5000*, www.grandhotelemerald.com. Although this five-star hotel is a bit off the beaten track, it makes up for it with a luxurious interior, the largest rooms of the city's five-star hotels, a gym, full spa and lovely atrium lounge. The area (not far from the Alexander Nevsky Lavra) is a bit quieter than the bustle on Nevsky.

Oktyabrskaya Hotel $$ *Ligovsky prospekt 10, tel: 812- 578-1515*, www. oktober-hotel.spb.ru. This hotel dating from the mid-19th century has been transformed from a rather fusty Soviet hotel into a modern place to lay your hat, though some of the past still remains. There are 373 rooms and all the usual amenities, several restaurants, bars and cafés and a fitness club. A good bargain in the city centre, although it may be a bit noisy.

Pushkinskaya 10 $$ *Ulitsa Pushinskaya 10, Apt 27, tel: 812-404 6148*, http://hotelsteam.ru. This nine-room mini-hotel is a little hard to find, since the neighbours in this rather elegant building did not want any signposts to mar their entrance (look instead for the discreet sign on the doorbell). But this bed and breakfast (accessed by a lift) is a real bargain, with a cheery kitchen, sauna and rooms in different styles, from modern to antique.

VASILEVSKY ISLAND

NashOtel (Our Hotel) $$$$ *11-aya liniya 50, tel: 812-323 2231*, www.nashotel.ru. If the Golden and Silver Ages of St Petersburg are not to your taste, you might enjoy NashOtel – a bright and modern anomaly among the city's largely retro hotel offerings. The hotel has 58 good-sized rooms filled with bright floral art, comfortable modern furnishings and bright-coloured sheets and pillows. It is located about five minutes from the Vasileostrovskaya metro station, near the Spit. Breakfast not included.

Sokos Hotel Vasilevsky $$$ *8-aya liniya 11/13, tel: 812-335 2290*, www. sokoshotels.com. A hop across the Blagovehchensky Bridge from the main sights, the Sokos Vasilevsky, belonging to the Finnish chain, has 255 well-designed rooms styled in sumptuous imperial fabrics, its own art gallery and the Repin Lounge Restaurant serving Russian favourites.

DICTIONARY

ENGLISH–RUSSIAN

adj adjective   **adv** adverb   **BE** British English   **n** noun   **prep** preposition   **v** verb

A

a few несколько _nyeh•skahl´•kah_
a little немного _nee•mnoh•gah_
a lot много _mnoh•gah_
a.m. до полудня _dah pah•lood•nyah_
about (approximately) около _oh•kah•lah_
abroad заграницей _zah•grah•nee•tsey_
accept v принимать _pree•nee•maht´_
access n допуск _doh•poosk_
accessories принадлежности _pree•nahd•lyezh•nah•stee_
accident несчастный случай _nee•shchas•niy sloo•chie;_ **(road)** авария _ah•vah•ree•yah_
accompany провожать _prah•vah•zhaht´_
accountant бухгалтер _boo•gahl•teer_
acetaminophen парацетамол _pah•rah•tsih•tah•mol_
acne прыщ _prihshch_
across через _cheh•rees_
adapter адаптер _ah•dahp•ter_
address адрес _ah•drees_
adhesive bandage пластырь _plahs•tihr´_
admission charge входная плата _fkhahd•nah•yah plah•tah_
adult взрослый _vzros•liy_
after после _pos•lee_

aftershave лосьон после бритья _las´•yon pos•lee breet´•yah_
age n возраст _voz•rahst_
agree соглашаться _sah•glah•shah•tsa_
air воздух _voz•dookh_
air conditioning кондиционер _kahn•dee•tsih•ah•nyer_
air mail авиапочта _ah•vee•ah•poch•tah_
air pump воздушный насос _vahz•doosh•niy nah•sos_
air sickness bag гигиенический пакет _gee•gee•ee•nee•chees•keey pah•kyet_
airport аэропорт _ah•eh•rah•port_
aisle seat место у прохода _myes•tah oo prah•khoh•dah_
alarm clock будильник _boo•deel´•neek_
allergy аллергия _ah•leer•gee•yah_
almost почти _pahch•tee_
alone один _ah•deen_
already уже _oo•zheh_
also также _tahg•zheh_
alter переделывать _pee•ree•dyeh•lih•vaht´_
aluminum foil фольга _fahl´•gah_
always всегда _fseeg•dah_
amazing поразительный _pah•rah•zee•teel´•niy_
ambassador посол _pah•sol_
ambulance скорая помощь _skoh•rah•yah poh•mahshch_

American adj американский _ah•mee•ree•kahn•skeey_
amount сумма _soo•mah_
anesthetic обезболивающее _ah•beez•boh•lee•vah•yoo•s hchee•yeh_
animal животное _zhih•vot•nah•yeh_
another другой _droo•goy_
antibiotic n антибиотик _ahn•tee•bee•oh•teek_
antique антикварный _ahn•tee•kvahr•niy_
antiques store антикварный магазин _ahn•tee•kvahr•niy mah•gah•zeen_
antiseptic n антисептик _ahn•tee•sep•teek_
any какой-либо _kah•koy•lee•bah_
anyone кто-нибудь _ktoh•nee•boot´_
anything что-нибудь _shtoh•nee•boot´_
apartment квартира _kvahr•tee•rah_
apologize просить прощения _prah•seet´ prah•shchen•nee•yah_
appendix аппендикс _ah•pyen•deeks_
appointment приём _pree•yom_
approximately приблизительно _pree•blee•zee•teel´•nah_
area code код _kot_
arm рука _roo•kah_

around (place) по *pah*; **(time)** около *oh•kah•lah*

arrive прибывать *pree•bih•vaht'*

art gallery картинная галерея *kahr•teen•nah•yah gah•leh•ryeh•yah*

ashtray пепельница *pyeh•peel'•nee•tsah*

ask просить *prah•seet'*

aspirin аспирин *ah•spee•reen*

asthmatic *n* астматик *ahst•mah•teek*

at в *v*

ATM банкомат *bahn•kah•maht*

attack *n* нападение *nah•pah•dyeh•nee•yeh*

attractive привлекательный *pree•vlee•kah•teel'•niy*

authentic настоящий *nah•stah•yah•shcheey*

authenticity подлинность *pod•leen•nahst'*

available (unoccupied) свободный *svah•bod•niy*

B

baby ребёнок *ree•byoh•nahk*

babysitter няня *nyah•nyah*

back спина *spee•nah*

backache боль в спине *bol' f spee•nyeh*

backpack рюкзак *ryoog•zahk*

bad плохой *plah•khoy*

baggage [BE] багаж *bah•gahzh*

baggage check багажная квитанция *bah•gahzh•nah•yah kvee•tahn•tsih•yah*

bakery булочная *boo•lahch•nah•yah*

balcony балкон *bahl•kon*

ball мяч *myahch*

ballet балет *bah•lyet*

band (musical group) группа *groo•pah*

bank банк *bahnk*

bar бар *bahr*

barber парикмахер *pah•reekh•mah•kheer*

basement подвал *pahd•vahl*

basket корзина *kahr•zee•nah*

basketball баскетбол *bahs•keet•bol*

battery (car) аккумулятор *ah•kah•moo•lyah•tahr*; **(camera, etc.)** батарея *bah•tah•ryeh•yah*

be быть *biht'*

beach пляж *plyahsh*

beautiful красивый *krah•see•viy*

because потому что *pah•tah•moo•shtah*

bed кровать *krah•vaht'*

bedding постельное бельё *pahs•tel'•nah•yeh beel'•yoh*

bedroom спальня *spahl'•nyah*

before (time) до *dah*

begin начинать *nah•chee•naht'*

belong принадлежать *pree•nahd•lee•zhaht'*

belt ремень *ree•myen'*

bicycle велосипед *vee•lah•see•pyet*

big большой *bahl'•shoy*

bikini бикини *bee•kee•nee*

bill счёт *shchot*

binoculars бинокль *bee•noh•kahl'*

bird птица *ptee•tsah*

birthday день рождения *dyen' rahzh•dyeh•nee•yah*

bite *n* укус *oo•koos*; *v* кусать *koo•saht'*

bizarre причудливый *pree•chood•lee•viy*

bladder мочевой пузырь *mah•chee•voy poo•zihr'*

blanket одеяло *ah•dee•yah•lah*

bleach отбеливатель *aht•byeh•lee•vah•teel'*

bleeding *n* кровотечение *krah•vah•tee•cheh•nee•yeh*

blister волдырь *vahl•dihr'*

blood кровь *krof*

blood pressure кровяное давление *krah•vee•noh•yeh dahv•lyeh•nee•yeh*

blouse блузка *bloos•kah*

blow-dry фен *fyen*

boarding card посадочный талон *pah•sah•dahch•niy tah•lon*

boat лодка *lot•kah*

boat trip водная экскурсия *vod•nah•yah ehks•koor•see•yah*

bone кость *kost'*

book *n* книга *knee•gah*; *v* заказывать *zah•kah•zih•vaht'*

bookstore книжный магазин *kneezh•niy mah•gah•zeen*

boots сапоги *sa•pah•gee*

borrow одолжить *ah•dahl•zhit'*

botanical garden ботанический сад *bah•tah•nee•chees•keey saht*

bottle opener открывалка *aht•krih•vahl•kah*

boy мальчик *mahl'•cheek*

boyfriend друг *drook*

bra бюстгальтер *byoost•gahl•tyer*

bracelet браслет *brahs•lyet*

break *v* сломать *slah•maht'*

break down *v* сломаться *slah•mah•tsah*

break-in *n* взлом *vzlom*

breast грудь *groot'*

breathe дышать *dih•shaht'*

breathtaking захватывающий *zah•khvah•tih•vah•yoo•shcheey*

bridge мост *most*

British *adj* британский *bree•tahn•skeey*

brochure брошюра
brah•shoo•rah
brooch брошь *brosh*
browse v просматривать
prah•smah•tree•vaht'
bruise *n* синяк *see•nyahk*
bucket ведро *veed•roh*
build строить *stroh•eet'*
building здание *zdah•nee•yeh*
burn *n* ожог *ah•zhok*
bus автобус *ahf•toh•boos*
bus route автобусный маршрут
ahf•toh•boos•niy mahrsh•root
bus station автобусная станция
*ahf•toh•boos•nah•yah
stahn•tsih•yah*
bus stop автобусная остановка
*ahf•toh•boos•nah•yah
ahs•tah•nof•kah*
business бизнес *beez•nees*
business trip командировка
kah•mahn•dee•rof•kah
busy *adj* (occupied) занятый
zah•nyah•tiy
but но *noh*
butane gas газовый баллон
gah•zah•viy bah•lon
button кнопка *knop•kah*
buy покупать *pah•koo•paht'*
by (time) к *k*

C

cabin каюта *kah•yoo•tah*
calendar календарь
kah•leen•dahr'
call v звать *zvaht';* (for
someone) заходить за
zah•khah•deet' zah; (phone)
звонить *zvah•neet'*
camera фотоаппарат
foh•tah•ah•pah•raht
camera case футляр *foot•lyahr*
campbed раскладушка
rahs•klah•doosh•kah
camping кемпинг *kyem•peenk*

**camping equip-
ment** снаряжение
snah•ree•zhen•nee•yeh
campsite палаточный лагерь
pah•lah•tahch•niy lah•geer'
can *n* банка *bahn•kahn;* v мочь
moch
can opener консервный нож
kahn•syerv•niy nosh
cancel отменять *aht•mee•nyaht'*
candle свеча *svee•chah*
cap (dental) коронка
kah•ron•kah
car машина *mah•shih•nah;*
(train compartment) вагон
vahh•gon
car hire [BE] прокат
автомобилей *prah•kaht
ahf•tah•mah•bee•leey*
car park [BE] автостоянка
ahf•tah•stah•yahn•kah
carafe графин *grah•feen*
careful осторожный
ahs•tah•rozh•niy
carpet (rug) ковер *kah•vyor*
cart тележка *tee•lyesh•kah*
carton пакет *pah•kyet*
cash наличные
nah•leech•nih•yeh
cash desk касса *kah•sah*
cashier кассир *kah•seer*
casino казино *kah•zee•noh*
castle замок *zah•mahk*
cathedral собор *sah•bor*
cave пещера *pee•shcheh•rah*
CD компакт-диск *kahm•pahkt
deesk*
CD player лазерный
проигрыватель *lah•zeer•niy
prah•eeg•rih•vah•teel'*
cell phone мобильный телефон
mah•beel'•niy tee•lee•fon
center центр *tsentr*
ceramics керамика
kee•rah•mee•kah

certificate свидетельство
svee•dyeh•teel'•stvah
chain цепочка *tsih•poch•kah*
change *n* сдача *zdah•chah;*
v (alter) поменять
pah•mee•nyaht'; (buses,
etc.) делать пересадку
dyeh•laht' pee•ree•saht•koo;
(baby) перепеленать
pee•ree•pee•lee•naht';
(money) обменять
ahb•mee•nyaht'
charge *n* плата *plah•tah*
charter flight чартерный рейс
chahr•ter•niy reys
cheap дешёвый *dee•shoh•viy*
check *n* чек *chek;* v проверять
prah•veh•ryaht'
check in v регистрироваться
ree•gees•tree•rah•vah•tsah
check-in desk регистрационная
стойка *ree•gee•strah•tsih•
on•nah•yah stoy•kah*
check out v (hotel) выезжать
vih•eezh•zhaht'
chemist [BE] аптека
ahp•tyeh•kah
cheque [BE] чек *chek*
chess шахматы *shahkh•mah•tih*
chest (body part) грудная клетка
grood•nah•yah klet•kah
child *adj* детский *dyets•keey;* *n*
ребёнок *ree•byon•nahk*
child seat (in car) детское
сиденье *dyets•kah•yeh
see•dyen'•yeh*
children дети *dyeh•teeh*
church церковь *tser•kahf'*
cigarette сигарета
see•gah•ryeh•tah
cigar сигара *see•gah•rah*
cinema [BE] кинотеатр
kee•nah•tee•ahtr
class (type of seat, etc.)
класс *klahs*

clean adj чистый _chees•tiy_; v
чистить _chees•teet'_

cliff скала _skah•lah_

cling film [BE]
продуктовая плёнка
_prah•dook•toh•vah•yah
plyon•kah_

clock часы _chah•sih_

close v (store, etc.)
закрываться
zah•krih•vah•tsah

clothes одежда _ah•dyezh•dah_

cloudy облачный _ob•lahch•niy_

clubs (golf) клюшки
klyoosh•kee

coach (long-distance bus)
междугородний автобус
_meezh•doo•gah•rod•niy
ahf•toh•boos_

coast побережье
pah•bee•ryezh•yeh

coat пальто _pahl'•toh_

coatcheck гардероб
gahr•dee•rop

code (area, dialing) код _kot_

coin монета _mah•nyeh•tah_

cold adj холодный _khah•lod•niy_;
n (flu) простуда
prah•stoo•dah

colleague коллега _kah•lyeh•gah_

collect v забирать _zah•bee•raht'_

color цвет _tsvyet_

comb расчёска _rah•shchos•kah_

come приходить _pree•khah•deet'_

commission комиссионный
сбор _kah•mee•see•oh•niy zbor_

compact компактный
kahm•pahk•tniy

company (busi-
ness) предприятие
preet•pree•yah•tee•yeh;
(companionship) компания
kahm•pah•nee•yah

compartment (train) купе
koo•peh

complaint жалоба _zhah•lah•bah_

concert концерт _kahn•tsert_

concert hall концертный зал
kahn•tsert•niy zahl

concussion сотрясение мозга
_sah•tree•syeh•nee•yeh
moz•gah_

conditioner кондиционер
kahn•dee•tsih•ah•nyer

condom презерватив
pree•zeer•vah•teev

conductor дирижёр
dee•ree•zhor

confirm (reservation)
подтвердить _paht•tveer•deet'_

consulate консульство
kon•sool'•stvah

consult v консультироваться
kahn•sool'•tee•rah•vah•tsah

contact v связаться
svyah•zah•tsah

contagious инфекционный
een•feek•tsih•oh•niy

contain v содержать
sah•deer•zhaht'

cook n повар _poh•vahr_; v
готовить _gah•toh•veet'_

cooker [BE] плита _plee•tah_

copper медь _myet'_

copy n копия _koh•pee•yah_

corkscrew штопор _shtoh•pahr_

corner угол _oo•gahl_

correct adv правильно
prah•veel'•nah

cosmetics косметика
kahs•myeh•tee•kah

cottage дача _dah•chah_

cotton вата _vah•tah_

cough n кашель _kah•shihl'_; v
кашлять _kahsh•lyaht'_

country (nation) страна
strah•nah

cramps судороги
soo•dah•rah•gee

credit card кредитная
карточка _kree•deet•nah•yah
kahr•tahch•kah_

crib детская кроватка
dets•kah•yah krah•vaht•kah

crossroad перекрёсток
pee•ree•kryos•tahk

cruise n круиз _kroo•eez_

crutches костыли _kahs•tih•lee_

crystal хрусталь _khroos•tal'_

cup чашка _chahsh•kah_

cupboard шкаф _shkaf_

currency валюта _vah•lyoo•tah_

currency exchange office
обмен валюты _ahb•myen
vah•lyoo•tih_

curtains занавеси
zah•nah•vee•see

customs таможня
tah•mozh•nyah

customs declaration
таможенная декларация
_tah•moh•zhih•nah•yah
deek•lah•rah•tsih•yah_

cut порез _pah•ryes_

cycle route велосипедный
маршрут _vee•lah•see•pyed•niy
mahrsh•root_

cycling велоспорт
vyeh•lah•sport

D

daily ежедневно
ee•zhee•dnyev•nah

damage v повредить
pah•vree•deet'

damp adv сыро _sih•rah_; n
сырость _sih•rahst'_

dance n танец _tah•neets_

dangerous adj опасный
ah•pahs•niy

dark тёмный _tyom•niy_

dawn рассвет _rahs•vyet_

day день _dyen'_

deaf глухой _gloo•khoy_

deck chair шезлонг _shez•lonk_

declare предъявлять
preed•*yav•l**yat***

deep глубокий gloo•*boh•keey*

degree (temperature) градус
grah•doos

delay задержка zah•*dyersh•kah*

deliver доставлять
dah•stahv•*lyat'*

denim джинсовый
dzhihn•*soh•viy*

dentist зубной врач zoob•*noy*
vrahch

dentures протез prah•*tes*

deodorant дезодорант
dee•zah•dah•*rahnt*

depart (train, bus)
отправляться
aht•prahv•*lyah•tsah*

department отдел aht•*dyel*

departure lounge зал вылета
zahl *vih•le•tah*

deposit аванс ah•*vahns*

describe описывать
ah•*pee•sih•vaht'*

destination место
назначения *myes•tah*
nahz•nah•*cheh•nee•yah*

details подробности
pahd•*rob•nahs•tee*

detergent моющее средство
*moh•*yoo•shchee•yeh
sryet•stvah*

diabetes диабет dee•ah•*byet*

diabetic n диабетик
dee•ah•*byeh•teek*

diagnosis диагноз
dee•*ahg•nahs*

diamond брильянт breel'•*yahnt*

diaper пелёнка pee•*lyon•kah*

diarrhea понос pah•*nos*

dice кости *kos•tee*

dictionary словарь slah•*vahr'*

diesel дизельное топливо
dee•zeel'•nah•yeh top•lee•vah

diet n диета dee•*yeh•tah*

difficult трудный *trood•niy*

dining car вагон-ресторан
vah•*gon* res•tah•*rahn*

dining room столовая
stah•*loh•vah•yah*

dinner ужин oo•*zhihn*

direct adj **(train)** прямой
pryah•*moy*; v направлять
nah•prahv•*lyat'*

direction направление
nah•prahv•*lyeh•nee•yeh*

director директор dee•*ryek•tahr*

directory (telephone)
телефонный справочник
tee•lee•*foh•niy*
sprah•vahch•neek

dirty грязный *gryahz•niy*

disabled инвалид een•vah•*leet*

discount скидка *skeet•kah*

dish (meal) блюдо *blyoo•dah*

dishcloth тряпка *tryahp•kah*

dishwasher посудомоечная
машина *pah•soo•dah•moh•*
eech•nah•yah mah•*shih•nah*

dishwashing liquid средство
для мытья посуды *sryet•stvah*
dlyah miht'•*yah* pah•*soo•dih*

disturb беспокоить
bees•pah•*koh•eet'*

dive нырять nih•*ryat'*

diving equipment
снаряжение для дайвинга
snah•ree•*zheh•nee•yeh* dlyah
die•veen•gah

divorce развод rahz•*vod*

doctor врач vrahch

doll кукла *kook•lah*

door дверь dvyer'

double bed двуспальная
кровать dvoo•*spahl'•*nah•yah
krah•*vaht'*

double room двухместный номер
dvookh•*myes•niy noh•*meer

downtown area центр города
tsentr *goh•rah•dah*

dozen дюжина *dyoo•zhih•nah*

dress платье *plaht'•yeh*

drink v пить peet'

drive v ехать yeh•*khaht'*

driver водитель vah•*dee•teel'*

driver's licence водительские
права vah•*dee•teel'•skee•ye*
prah•vah

drugstore аптека ahp•*tyeh•*kah

drunk adj пьяный *pyah•niy*

dry clean v отдавать в
химчистку aht•dah•*vaht'* f
kheem•*cheest•koo*

dry cleaner химчистка
kheem•*cheest•kah*

during во время vah *vrye•myah*

dustbin [BE] мусорный бак
moo•sahr•niy bank

duty пошлина *posh•lee•nah*

E

ear ухо *oo•khah*

earache боль в ухе bol' v
oo•khee

early ранний *rahn•neey*

earrings серьги *syer'•*gee

easy лёгкий *lyokh•keey*

eat есть yest'

economy class пассажирский
класс pah•sah•*zhihr•skeey*
klahs

electric outlet розетка
rah•*zyet•kah*

electric shaver электробритва
eh•*lyek•trah•breet•*vah

electricity электричество
eh•leek•*tree•cheest•vah*

elevator лифт leeft

else ещё ee•*shchoh*

e-mail электронная почта
eh•leek•*troh•nah•yah*
poch•tah

e-mail address адрес
электронной почты *ah•*drees
ee•leek•*tron•nie poch•tih*

e-ticket электронный билет
ee•leek•<u>tron</u>•niy bee•<u>lyet</u>

embassy посольство
pah•<u>sol</u>•stvah

emerald изумруд ee•zoom•<u>root</u>

emergency крайний случай
<u>krie</u>•neey sloo•chie

emergency exit аварийный
выход ah•vah•<u>reey</u>•niy
vih•khaht

empty adj пустой poos•<u>toy</u>

enamel эмаль ee•<u>mahl'</u>

end v кончаться kahn•<u>chah</u>•tsah

England Англия <u>ahn</u>•glee•yah

English adj английский
ahn•<u>gleey</u>•skeey

enjoy нравиться <u>nrah</u>•vee•tsah

enough достаточно
dah•<u>stah</u>•tahch•nah

entrance fee входная плата
fkhahd•<u>nah</u>•yah <u>plah</u>•tah

entry visa въездная виза
vyezd•<u>nah</u>•yah vee•zah

envelope конверт kahn•<u>vyert</u>

epileptic n эпилептик
ee•pee•<u>lyep</u>•teek

equipment оборудование
ah•bah•<u>roo</u>•dah•vah•nee•yeh;
(sports) снаряжение
snah•<u>ryah</u>•<u>zheh</u>•nee•yeh

error ошибка ah•<u>shihp</u>•kah

escalator эскалатор
ees•kah•<u>lah</u>•tahr

essential основной ahs•nahv•<u>noy</u>

European Union (EU)
Европейский союз
yev•rah•<u>pey</u>•skeey sah•<u>yoos</u>

event событие sah•<u>bih</u>•tee•yeh

every каждый <u>kahzh</u>•diy

example пример pree•<u>myer</u>

except кроме <u>kroh</u>•meh

excess luggage перевес багажа
pee•ree•<u>vyes</u> bah•gah•<u>zhah</u>

exchange v обменивать
ahb•<u>myeh</u>•nee•vaht'

exchange rate курс обмена
koors ahb•<u>myeh</u>•nah

excursion экскурсия
eks•<u>koor</u>•see•yah

exit n выход <u>vih</u>•khaht

expensive дорогой dah•rah•<u>goy</u>

express экспресс eks•<u>pres</u>

extension добавочный номер
dah•<u>bah</u>•vahch•niy <u>noh</u>•meer

extra adv ещё ee•<u>shchoh</u>

extract v удалять oo•dah•<u>lyaht'</u>

eye глаз glahs

fabric (material) ткань tkahn'

face лицо lee•<u>tsoh</u>

facial чистка лица <u>cheest</u>•kah
lee•<u>tsah</u>

facilities удобства oo•<u>dops</u>•tvah

family семья seem'•<u>yah</u>

fan (air) вентилятор
veen•tee•<u>lyah</u>•tahr

far далеко dah•lee•<u>koh</u>

far-sighted дальнозоркий
dahl'•nah•<u>zor</u>•keey

fare плата <u>plah</u>•tah

farm ферма <u>fyer</u>•mah

fast adv быстро <u>bihst</u>•rah

faucet кран krahn

favorite любимый lyoo•<u>bee</u>•miy

fax факс faks

feed кормить kar•<u>meet'</u>

ferry паром pah•<u>rom</u>

fever жар zhahr

few мало <u>mah</u>•lah

filling (dental) пломба
<u>plom</u>•bah

film [BE] (movie) фильм feel'm;
(camera) плёнка <u>plyon</u>•kah

filter фильтр <u>feel'</u>•tr

finger палец <u>pah</u>•leets

fire n пожар pah•<u>zhahr</u>

fire alarm пожарная тревога
pah•<u>zhahr</u>•nah•yah
tree•<u>voh</u>•gah

fire escape пожарная
лестница pah•<u>zhahr</u>•nah•yah
<u>lyes</u>•nee•tsah

fire extinguisher огнетушитель
ahg•nee•<u>too</u>•<u>shih</u>•teel'

firewood дрова drah•<u>vah</u>

first class первый класс
<u>pyer</u>•viy klahs

fit v **(clothes)** подходить
paht•khah•<u>deet'</u>

fitting room примерочная
pree•<u>myeh</u>•rahch•nah•yah

fix v чинить chee•<u>neet'</u>

flashlight фонарь fah•<u>nahr'</u>

flight рейс reys

floor этаж eh•<u>tahsh</u>

florist цветочный магазин
tsvyeh•<u>toch</u>•niy mah•gah•<u>zeen</u>

flower цветок tsvee•<u>tok</u>

flu грипп greep

fog туман too•<u>mahn</u>

folk народный nah•<u>rod</u>•niy

follow v **(pursue)** преследовать
pree•<u>slyeh</u>•dah•vaht'

food n еда yee•<u>dah</u>

foot (body) нога nah•<u>gah</u>

football [BE] футбол foot•<u>bol</u>

footpath тропинка trah•<u>peen</u>•kah

for на nah

foreign currency иностранная
валюта ee•nah•<u>strah</u>•nah•yah
vah•<u>lyoo</u>•tah

forest лес lyes

forget забывать zah•bih•<u>vaht'</u>

fork вилка <u>veel</u>•kah

form n бланк blahnk

fountain фонтан fahn•<u>tahn</u>

foyer (hotel, theater) фойе
fie•<u>yeh</u>

fracture (a bone) перелом
pee•ree•<u>lom</u>

frame n **(glasses)** оправа
ah•<u>prah</u>•vah

free adj **(not busy/available)**
свободный svah•<u>bod</u>•niy

freezer морозильная камера
*mah•rah•zeel'•nah•yah
kah•mee•rah*
frequently часто *chahs•tah*
fresh свежий *svyeh•zhiy*
friend друг *drook*
friendly *adj* дружеский
droo•zhees•keey
from (place) из *eez*; **(time)** с *s*
frost мороз *mah•roz*
frying pan сковорода
skah•vah•rah•dah
full *adj* полный *pol•niy*
fun веселье *vee•syel'•yeh*
furniture мебель *myeh•beel'*

G

game игра *eeg•rah*
garage гараж *gah•rash*
garbage bag мусорный мешок
moo•sahr•niy mee•shok
garden сад *saht*
gas (fuel) бензин *been•zeen*
gas station
заправочная станция
*zah•prah•vahch•nah•yah
stahn•tsih•yah*
gate (airport) выход *vih•khaht*
gauze бинт *beent*
genuine настоящий
nah•stah•yah•shcheey
get (receive) получать
pah•loo•chaht'; **(to
destination)** добираться до
dah•bee•rah•tsah doh
gift подарок *pah•dah•rahk*
gift store магазин подарков
mah•gah•zeen pah•dahr•kahf
girl девочка *dyeh•vahch•kah*
girlfriend подруга
pah•droo•gah
give давать *dah•vaht'*
glass стакан *stah•kahn*
glasses (optical) очки
ahch•kee

glove перчатка *peer•chaht•kah*
go ходить *khah•deet'*
go away уходить *oo•khah•deet'*
gold золото *zoh•lah•tah*
golf гольф *gol'f*
golf course поле для гольфа
poh•lyeh dlyah gol'•fah
good хороший *khah•roh•shiy*
gram грамм *grahm*
grass трава *trah•vah*
gray серый *syeh•riy*
Great Britain Великобритания
*vee•lee•kah•bree•tah•
nee•yah*
group группа *groo•pah*
guarantee гарантия
gah•rahn•tee•yah
guide (tour) гид *geet*
guidebook путеводитель
poo•tee•vah•dee•teel'
guided tour экскурсия
eks•koor•see•yah
guitar гитара *gee•tah•rah*
gum десна *dees•nah*
gym спортзал *sport•zahl*
gynecologist гинеколог
gee•nee•koh•lahk

H

hair волосы *voh•lah•sih*
hairbrush щётка для волос
shchot•kah dlyah vah•los
haircut стрижка *streesh•kah*
hairdresser парикмахер
pah•reek•mah•kheer
hairspray лак для волос *lahk
dlyah vah•los*
half половина
pah•lah•vee•nah
hand рука *roo•kah*
hand luggage ручная кладь
rooch•nah•yah klahd'
handbag [BE] сумка *soom•kah*
handicapped инвалид
een•vah•leet

handicraft ремесло
ree•mees•loh
handkerchief платок *plah•tok*
hanger вешалка *vyeh•shahl•kah*
hangover похмелье
pahkh•myel'•yeh
harbor гавань *gah•vahn'*
hat шапка *shahp•kah*
hay fever сенная
лихорадка *see•nah•yah
lee•khah•raht•kah*
head голова *gah•lah•vah*
headache головная боль
gah•lahv•nah•yah bol'
health insurance
медицинское страхование
*mee•dee•tsihn•skah•yah
strah•khof•kah*
hear слышать *slih•shaht'*
hearing aid слуховой аппарат
sloo•khah•voy ah•pah•raht
heart сердце *syer•tseh*
heart attack сердечный
приступ *seer•dyech•niy
prees•toop*
heart condition
заболевание сердца
*zah•bah•lee•vah•nee•yeh
syer•tsah*
heater обогреватель
ah•bah•gree•vah•teel'
heating *n* отопление
ah•tahp•lyeh•nee•yeh
heavy тяжёлый *tee•zhoh•liy*
height рост *rost*
helmet шлем *shlyem*
help *v* помогать *pah•mah•gaht'*
here здесь *zdyes'*
high высокий *vih•soh•keey*
high blood pressure высокое
давление *vih•soh•kha•yeh
dahv•lyeh•nee•yeh*
highlight *v* (hair) мелировать
mee•lee•rah•vaht'
highway шоссе *shah•seh*

hiking n поход pah•_khot_
hill холм kholm
hire [BE] v взять напрокат
vzyaht' nah•prah•_kaht_
hobby хобби _khoh_•bee
hold on v подождать
bah•dah•_zhdaht'_
hole (in clothes) дырка
dihr•kah
holiday [BE] отпуск ot•poosk
home дом dom
honeymoon медовый месяц
mee•_doh_•viy myeh•syahts
horse лошадь _loh_•shahd'
horseracing бега bee•_gah_
hospital больница
bahl'•_nee_•tsah
hot adj горячий gah•_ryah_•cheey
hotel гостиница
gahs•_tee_•nee•tsah
hotel room номер _noh_•meer
hour час chahs
house дом dom
hungry голодный gah•_lod_•niy
hurt v болеть bah•_lyet'_
husband муж moosh

I

icy гололёд gah•lah•_lyot_
identification документ
dah•koo•_myent_
ill [BE] больной bahl'•_noy_
illegal незаконный
nee•zah•_koh_•niy
immediately немедленно
nee•_myeh_•dlee•nah
in (place) в v; **(time)** через
cheh•rees
incredible невероятный
nee•vee•rah•_yaht_•niy
indigestion изжога
eezh•_zhoh_•gah
indoor закрытый zah•_krih_•tiy
inexpensive недорогой
nee•dah•rah•_goy_

infect заразить zah•rah•_zeet'_
infection инфекция
een•_fyek_•tsih•yah
inflammation воспаление
vahs•pah•_lyeh_•nee•yeh
information информация
een•fahr•_mah_•tsih•yah
injection укол oo•_kol_
injury травма _trahv_•mah
innocent невиновен
nee•vee•_noh_•veen
insect насекомое
nah•see•_koh_•mah•yeh
insert v вставлять fstahv•_lyat'_
inside внутри vnoo•_tree_
insist настаивать
nah•_stah_•ee•vaht'
insomnia бессоница
bees•_soh_•nee•tsah
instructions инструкция
een•_strook_•tsih•yah
insulin инсулин een•soo•_leen_
insurance страховка
strah•_khof_•kahh
insurance claim страховой иск
strah•khah•_voy_ eesk
insurance company страховая
компания strah•khah•_vah_•yah
kahm•_pah_•nee•yah
interesting интересный
een•tee•_ryes_•niy
internet интернет een•ter•_net_
internet cafe интернет-кафе
een•ter•_net_ kah•_feh_
interpreter переводчик
pee•ree•_vot_•cheek
intersection перекресток
pee•ree•_kryos_•tahk
invitation приглашение
pree•glah•_sheh_•nee•yeh
invite приглашать
pree•glah•_shaht'_
iron утюг oo•_tyook_
itemized bill детальный счёт
dee•_tahl'_•niy shchot

J

jacket куртка _koort_•kah
jar банка _bahn_•kah
jaw челюсть cheh•_lyoost'_
jazz джаз dzhahs
jeans джинсы _dzhihn_•sih
jeweler ювелирный
магазин yoo•vee•_leer_•niy
mah•gah•_zeen_
job работа rah•_boh_•tah
joke шутка _shoot_•kah
journalist журналист
zhoor•nah•_leest_
journey поездка pah•_yest_•kah

K

kettle чайник _chie_•neek
key ключ klyooch
key card электронный ключ
eh•_leek_•_tron_•niy klyooch
key ring брелок bree•_lok_
kiddie pool детский бассейн
dyets•keey bah•_seyn_
kidney почка _poch_•kah
kind (pleasant) любезный
lyoo•_byez_•niy
kiss v целовать tsih•lah•_vaht'_
kitchen кухня _kookh_•nyah
knee колено kah•_lyeh_•nah
knife нож nosh
kosher кошерный kah•_sher_•niy

L

label n ярлык yahr•_lihk_
lace кружево kroo•_zhih_•vah
ladder стремянка
stree•_myahn_•kah
lake озеро oh•_zee_•rah
lamp лампа _lahm_•pah
land v приземляться
pree•zeem•_lyah_•tsah
language course языковые
курсы yah•zih•kah•_vih_•yeh
koor•sih
large большой bahl'•_shoy_

last *adj* последний
pahs•lyed•neey
late *adj* поздний *poz•neey*
laugh *v* смеяться *smee•yah•tsah*
launderette [BE] прачечная
prah•cheech•nah•yah
laundromat прачечная
prah•cheech•nah•yah
lawyer адвокат *ahd•vah•kaht*
leader (of group) руководитель
roo•kah•vah•dee•teel'
leaflet брошюра *brah•shoo•rah*
leak *v* (roof, pipe) течь *tyech*
learn (language) изучать
ee•zoo•chaht'
leather кожа *koh•zhah*
leave *v* уезжать *oo•eezh•zhaht'*
left *adj* левый *leh•viy*
left-luggage office [BE] камера хранения *kah•mee•rah khrah•nyeh•nee•yah*
leg нога *nah•gah*
legal законный *zah•koh•niy*
lend дать взаймы *daht' vzie•mih*
length длина *dlee•nah*
less меньше *myen'•sheh*
lesson урок *oo•rok*
letter письмо *pees'•moh*
library библиотека
bee•blee•ah•tyeh•kah
lifeboat спасательная лодка
spah•sah•teel'•nah•yah lot•kah
lifeguard спасатель
spah•sah•teel'
lifejacket спасательный жилет
spah•sah•teel'•niy zhih•lyet
lift [BE] *n* лифт *leeft*
lift pass пропуск на подъёмник *proh•poosk nah pahd•yom•neek*
light *adj* (weight) лёгкий
lyokh•keey; (color) светлый
svyet•liy; (electric) свет *svyet*
light bulb лампочка
lahm•pahch•kah

lighter (cigarette) зажигалка
zah•zhih•gahl•kah
like *v* нравиться *nrah•vee•tsah*
line (subway) линия
lee•nee•yah
linen лён *lyon*
lip губа *goo•bah*
lipstick губная памада
goob•nah•yah pah•mah•dah
liquor store винный магазин
vee•niy mah•gah•zeen
little (small) маленький
mah•leen'•keey
liver печень *pyeh•cheen'*
living room гостиная
gahs•tee•nah•yah
lobby (theater, hotel) фойе
fah•yeh
local местный *mes•niy*
lock *n* замок *zah•mok*
login вход в систему *fhot f sees•tyeh•moo*
long длинный *dlee•niy*
long-distance bus междугородний автобус *myezh•doo•gah•rod•niy ahf•toh•boos*
long-sighted [BE] дальнозоркий
dahl'•nah•zor•keey
loose (clothing) свободный
svah•bod•niy
lose потерять *pah•tee•ryaht'*
lost-and-found бюро находок
byoo•roh nah•khoh•dahk
loud громкий *grom•keey*
love *v* любить *lyoo•beet'*
luggage багаж *bah•gahsh*
lunch обед *ah•byet*
lung лёгкое *lyokh•kah•yeh*

M

magazine журнал *zhoor•nahl*
magnificent великолепный
vee•lee•kah•lyep•niy

mail *n* почта *poch•tah*; *v* отправлять *aht•prahv•lyaht'*
mailbox почтовый ящик
pahch•toh•viy yah•shcheek
main главный *glahv•niy*
main course второе
ftah•roh•yeh
make-up макияж
mah•kee•yahsh
male мужской *moosh•skoy*
mall (shopping) торговый центр *tahr•goh•viy tsentr*
man (male) мужчина
moo•shchee•nah
manicure маникюр
mah•nee•kyoor
manual *n* (for smth)
руководство
roo•kah•vod•stvah
many много *mnoh•gah*
map карта *kahr•tah*
market рынок *rih•nahk*
married (man) женат
zhih•naht; (woman) замужем
zah•moo•zhem
mascara тушь *toosh*
mask (diving) маска
mahs•kah
massage массаж *mah•sahsh*
match (sport) матч *mahch*
matches спички *speech•kee*
mattress матрас *maht•rahs*
meal блюдо *blyoo•dah*
mean *v* значить *znah•cheet'*
measure *v* измерить
eez•myeh•reet'
measurement измерение
eez•mee•ryeh•nee•yeh
medication лекарство
lee•kahr•stvah
meet *v* встречаться
fstree•chah•tsah
message сообщение
sah•ahp•shcheh•nee•yeh
metal металл *mee•tahl*

microwave микроволновая печь
meek•rah•vahl•noh•vah•yah pyech
migraine мигрень *meeg•ryen'*
mileage километраж
kee•lah•mee•trahsh
mine мой *moy*
minute минута *mee•noo•tah*
mirror зеркало *zyer•kah•lah*
miss v **(pass)** пропустить
prah•poos•teet'; **(get lost)**
пропасть *prah•pahst'*
mistake ошибка *ah•shihp•kah*
misunderstanding
недоразумение *nee•dah•rah•zoo•myeh•nee•yeh*
mobile phone [BE] мобильный
телефон *mah•beel'•niy tee•lee•fon*
modern современный
sah•vree•myen•niy
money деньги *dyen'•gee*
month месяц *myeh•syahts*
mop швабра *shvahb•rah*
more больше *bol'•sheh*
mosque мечеть *mee•chet'*
mosquito bite комариный укус
kah•mah•ree•niy oo•koos
motion sickness морская
болезнь *mahr•skah•yah bah•lyezn'*
motorboat моторка
mah•tor•kah
motorway [BE] шоссе
shah•seh
mountain гора *gah•rah*
mouth рот *rot*
movie фильм *feel'm*
movie theater кинотеатр
kee•nah•tee•ahtr
Mr. господин *gahs•pah•deen*
Mrs. госпожа *gahs•pah•zhah*
much много *mnoh•gah*
mug n кружка *kroosh•kah*; v
ограбить *ah•grah•beet'*

mugging n ограбление
ah•grahb•lyeh•nee•yeh
museum музей *moo•zyey*
music музыка *moo•zih•kah*
my мой *moy*
myself сам *sahm*

N

name (first name) имя
ee•myah; **(family name)**
фамилия *fah•mee•lee•yah*
napkin салфетка *sahl•fyet•kah*
nappy [BE] пелёнка
pee•lyon•kah
narrow узкий *oos•keey*
national национальный
nah•tsih•ah•nahl'•niy
nationality национальность
nah•tsih•ah•nahl'•nahst'
nature reserve заповедник
zah•pah•vyed•neek
near около *oh•kah•lah*
nearby рядом *ryah•dahm*
near-sighted близорукий
blee•zа•roo•keey
neck шея *sheh•yah*
necklace ожерелье
ah•zhih•ryel'•yeh
nerve нерв *nyerf*
nesting doll матрёшка
maht•ryosh•kah
never никогда *nee•kahg•dah*
new новый *noh•viy*
newspaper газета
gah•zyeh•tah
newsstand газетный киоск
gah•zyet•niy kee•osk
next следующий
slyeh•doo•yoo•shcheey
nice хороший *khah•roh•shiy*
niece племянница
plee•myah•nee•tsah
no нет *nyet*
no one никто *nee•ktoh*
noisy шумный *shoom•niy*

non-alcoholic безалкогольный
beez•ahl•kah•gol'•niy
non-smoking некурящий
nee•koo•ryah•shcheey
nonsense ерунда *ee•roon•dah*
normal нормальный
nahr•mahl'•niy
nose нос *nos*
nothing ничего *nee•chee•voh*
notify сообщать
sah•ahp•shchaht'
number (phone) номер
noh•meer
nurse сестра *sees•trah*

O

occupied занятый *zah•nee•tiy*
odds (betting) шансы *shahn•sih*
off-license [BE] винный
магазин *vee•niy mah•gah•zeen*
office офис *oh•fees*
often часто *chahs•tah*
old старый *sta•riy*
on (day, date) в v; **(place)**
на *nah*
once один раз *ah•deen rahs*
one-way ticket билет в один
конец *bee•lyet v ah•deen kah•nyets*
open adj открытый *aht•krih•tiy*;
v открывать *aht•krih•vaht'*
opening hours часы работы
chah•sih rah•boh•tih
opera опера *oh•pee•rah*
operation операция
ah•pee•rah•tsih•yah
opposite напротив
nah•proh•teef
optician оптика *op•tee•kah*
or или *ee•lee*
orchestra оркестр *ahr•kyestr*
order v заказывать
zah•ka•zih•vaht'
ordering заказ *zah•kahs*

Orthodox православный
prah•vah•slahv•niy
other другой *droo•goy*
outdoor на открытом воздухе *nah aht•krih•tahm voz•doo•khee*
outside на улице *nah oo•lee•tseh*
oven духовка *doo•khof•kah*
overheat перегреться
pee•ree•gryeh•tsah
overlook *n* смотровая площадка *smah•trah•vah•yah plah•shchaht•kah*
owner владелец *vlah•dyeh•leets*

P

pacifier соска *sos•kah*
pack *v* упаковывать
oo•pah•koh•vih•vaht'
package посылка *pah•sihl•kah*
packet пакет *pah•kyet*
paddling pool [BE] детский бассейн *dyets•keey bah•seyn*
pain боль *bol'*
painkiller болеутоляющее *bo•h•lee•oo•tah•lyah•yoo•sh chee•yeh*
painting картина *kahr•tee•nah*
pair пара *pah•rah*
palace дворец *dvah•ryets*
panorama панорама
pah•nah•rah•mah
pants брюки *bryoo•kee*
paper бумага *boo•mah•gah*
paracetamol [BE] парацетамол
pah•rah•tsih•tah•mol
parents родители
rah•dee•tee•lee
park парк *pahrk*
parking lot автостоянка
ahf•tah•stah•yahn•kah
party (social) вечеринка
vee•chee•reen•kah
pass *v* проезжать
prah•eezh•zhaht'

passport паспорт *pahs•pahrt*
pastry store кондитерская
kahn•dee•teer•skah•yah
patch *v* заштопать *zah•shtoh•paht'*
path тропинка *trah•peen•kah*
patient *n* пациент *pah•tsih•yent*
pay *v* платить *plah•teet'*
pay phone телефон-автомат
tee•lee•fon ahf•tah•maht
payment оплата *ah•plah•tah*
peak пик *peek*
pearl жемчуг *zhem•chook*
pedestrian crossing переход
pee•ree•khot
pedestrian zone пешеходная зона *pee•shih•khod•nah•yah zoh•nah*
pedicure педикюр
pee•dee•kyoor
pen ручка *rooch•kah*
pencil карандаш
kah•rahn•dahsh
people люди *lyoo•dee*
perhaps может быть *moh•zhiht biht'*
period *n* (historical) период *pee•ree•aht*;
(menstrual) менструация
meen•stroo•ah•tsih•yah
petrol [BE] бензин *been•zeen*
pharmacy аптека *ahp•tyeh•kah*
phone *v* звонить *zvah•neet'*
phone card телефонная карточка *tee•lee•foh•nah•yah kahr•tahch•kah*
phone call звонок *zvah•nok*
photo фотография
fah•tah•grah•fee•yah
photocopier ксерокс
ksyeh•rahks
photography фотография
fah•tah•grah•fee•yah
phrase фраза *frah•zah*
phrase book разговорник
rahz•gah•vor•neek

pick up *v* (get) взять *vzyat'*;
(collect) забирать
zah•bee•raht'
picnic пикник *peek•neek*
piece *n* кусочек *koo•soh•cheek*
pill таблетка *tahb•lyet•kah*
pillow подушка *pah•doosh•kah*
pipe (smoking) трубка
troop•kah
piste трасса *trah•sah*
pizzeria пиццерия
pee•tsih•ree•yah
place (space) место *myes•tah*
plane самолёт *sah•mah•lyot*
plan план *plahn*
plant *n* растение
rahs•tyeh•nee•yeh
plastic bag пакет *pah•kyet*
plastic wrap
продуктовая плёнка
prah•dook•toh•vah•yah plyon•kah
plate тарелка *tah•rel•kah*
platform [BE] платформа
plaht•for•mah
platinum платина
plah•tee•nah
play *n* игра *eeg•rah*; *v* (games, etc.) играть *eeg•raht'*;
(perform) исполнять
ees•pahl•nyaht'
playground детская площадка *dyets•kah•yah plah•shchaht•kah*
playpen манеж *mah•nyesh*
pleasant приятный
pree•yaht•niy
please пожалуйста
pah•zhahl•stah
plug штепсель *shtep•seel'*
plunger вантуз *vahn•toos*
point *v* (at) показывать (на)
pah•kah•zih•vaht' (nah)
poison *n* яд *yaht*
poles палки *pahl•kee*

police милиция
mee•lee•tsih•yah
police station
отделение милиции
*aht•dee•lyeh•nee•yeh
mee•lee•tsih•ee*
popular популярный
pah•poo•lyahr•niy
port (harbor) порт *port*
porter носильщик
nah•seel•shcheek
portion порция *por•tsih•yah*
possible возможно
vahz•mozh•nah
post n почта *poch•tah;* v
отправлять *aht•prahv•lyaht'*
postbox [BE] почтовый ящик
pahch•toh•viy yah•shcheek
postcard открытка
aht•kriht•kah
pottery керамика
kee•rah•mee•kah
pound (sterling) фунт *foont*
pregnant беременная
bee•reh•mee•nah•yah
prescribe выписывать
vih•pee•sih•vaht'
prescription рецепт *ree•tsept*
present n (gift) подарок
pah•dah•rahk
press v гладить *glah•deet'*
pretty красивый *krah•see•viy*
print v печатать *pee•chah•taht'*
program n программа
prah•grah•mah
pronounce v произносить
prah•eez•nah•seet'
pump насос *nah•sos*
puncture прокол *prah•kol*
puppet show кукольный театр
koo•kahl'•niy tee•ahtr
pure (material) чистый
chees•tiy
purpose цель *tsel'*
purse сумка *soom•kah*

pushchair [BE]
прогулочная коляска
*prah•goo•lahch•nah•yah
kah•lyas•kah*
put v поставить *pah•stah•veet'*

Q

quality качество *kah•chees•tvah*
queue [BE] v стоять в очереди
stah•yaht' v oh•chee•ree•dee
quick быстрый *bihs•triy*
quiet тихий *tee•kheey*

R

racetrack ипподром
ee•pah•drom
racket (tennis) ракетка
rah•kyet•kah
railroad железная дорога
*zhee•lyez•nah•yah
dah•roh•gah*
railway [BE] железная
дорога *zhee•lyez•nah•yah
dah•roh•gah*
rain v идёт дождь *ee•dyot
doshch*
raincoat плащ *plahshch*
rape n изнасилование
eez•nah•see•lah•vah•nee•yeh
rapids пороги *pah•roh•gee*
rash сыпь *sihp'*
razor бритва *breet•vah*
read v читать *chee•taht'*
ready готовый *gah•toh•viy*
real (genuine) настоящий
nah•stah•yah•shcheey
receipt квитанция
kvee•tahn•tsih•yah
reception (desk) регистрация
ree•gee•strah•tsih•yah
receptionist портье *pahrt'•yeh*
recommend рекомендовать
ree•kah•meen•dah•vaht'
reduction (in price) скидка
skeet•kah

refrigerator холодильник
khah•lah•deel'•neek
refund вернуть деньги
veer•noot' dyen'•gee
region район *rah•yon*
regular adj (size) средний
sryed•neey
religion религия
ree•lee•gee•yah
remember помнить *pom•neet'*
rent v взять напрокат *vzyat'
nah•prah•kaht*
repair v чинить *chee•neet'*
repeat v повторять
pahf•tah•ryaht'
report v заявить *zah•yah•veet'*
reservation заказ *zah•kahs*
reserve v заказать *zah•kah•zaht'*
rest v отдыхать *aht•dih•khaht'*
restaurant ресторан
rees•tah•rahn
restroom туалет *too•ah•lyet*
retail торговля *tahr•gov•lya*
retired на пенсии *nah
pyen•see•ee*
return (surrender) возвратить
vahz•vrah•teet'
return ticket [BE] билет туда
и обратно *bee•lyet too•dah ee
ahb•raht•nah*
revolting отвратительный
aht•vrah•tee•teel'•niy
rib ребро *reeb•roh*
right adj (correct) правильный
prah•veel'•niy
ring кольцо *kahl'•tsoh*
river река *ree•kah*
road дорога *dah•roh•gah*
road map карта дорог *kahr•tah
dah•rok*
robbery грабеж *grah•byosh*
romantic романтичный
rah•mahn•teech•niy
roof (house, car) крыша
krih•shah

room комната _kom•nah•tah_
room service
обслуживание номеров
_ahp•<u>sloo</u>•zhih•vah•nee•yeh
nah•mee•rof_
rope веревка _vee•ryof•kah_
round adj круглый _kroog•liy;_ n
(of game) раунд _rah•oond_
round-trip ticket билет туда и
обратно _bee•<u>lyet</u> too•<u>dah</u> ee
ahb•<u>raht</u>•nah_
rubbish [BE] мусор _moo•sahr_
ruble [trouble] рубль _roobl'_
Russia Россия _rahs•<u>see</u>•yah_
Russian adj русский _roos•keey_
Russian language русский
язык _roos•kee yah•<u>zihk</u>_

s

safe adj безопасный
bee•zah•<u>pahs</u>•niy; n сейф _seyf_
safety безопасность
bee•zah•<u>pahs</u>•nahst'
safety pin булавка
boo•<u>laht</u>•kah
sailboat яхта _yahkh•tah es_
sales tax НДС _en deh es_
same тот же самый _tot zheh
<u>sah</u>•miy_
sand песок _pee•<u>sok</u>_
sandals сандалии _sahn•<u>dah</u>•lee_
sandy beach песчаный пляж
pee•<u>shchah</u>•niy plyahsh
sanitary napkins
гигиенические салфетки
_gee•gee•ee•<u>nee</u>•chees•
kee•yeh sahl•<u>fyet</u>•kee_
saucepan кастрюля
kahs•<u>tryoo</u>•lyah
sauna сауна _sah•oo•nah_
say v говорить _gah•vah•<u>reet'</u>_
scarf шарф _shahrf_
scenic route живописный
маршрут _zhi•vah•<u>pees</u>•niy
mahrsh•<u>root</u>_

schedule n расписание
rahs•pee•<u>sah</u>•nee•yeh
scissors ножницы
<u>nozh</u>•nee•tsih
screwdriver отвёртка
aht•<u>vyort</u>•kah
sea море _moh•ryeh_
seat место _myes•tah_
second class (train) купейный
вагон _koo•<u>pey</u>•niy vah•<u>gon</u>_
second-hand подержанный
pah•<u>dyer</u>•zhah•niy
secretary секретарь
seek•ree•<u>tahr'</u>
sedative успокаивающее _oo
s•pah•<u>kah</u>•ee•vah•yoo•sh
chee•yeh_
see видеть _vee•<u>deet'</u>_
self-service самообслуживание
_sah•mah•ahp•<u>sloo</u>•zhih•vah
•nee•yeh_
sell продавать _prah•dah•<u>vaht'</u>_
send посылать _pah•sih•<u>laht'</u>_
senior citizen пенсионер
pyen•see•ah•<u>nyer</u>
separately отдельно
ahd•<u>del</u>•nah
serious серьёзный _see•<u>ryoz</u>•niy_
service (religious)
служба _sloozh•bah;_ **(in
restaurant)** обслуживание
ahp•<u>sloo</u>•zhih•vah•nee•yeh
shade тень _tyen'_
shallow мелкий _myel•keey_
shampoo шампунь
shahm•<u>poon'</u>
shape n форма _for•mah_
share v **(a room)** делить
dee•<u>leet'</u>
sheet (bedding) простыня
prahs•tih•<u>nyah</u>
ship корабль _kah•<u>rahbl'</u>_
shirt рубашка _roo•<u>bahsh</u>•kah_
shoe repair ремонт обуви
ree•<u>mont</u> oh•boo•vee

shoe store обувной магазин
ah•boov•<u>noy</u> mah•gah•<u>zeen</u>
shoes туфли _toof•lee_
shop магазин _mah•gah•<u>zeen</u>_
shop assistant продавец
prah•dah•<u>vyets</u>
shopping basket корзинка
kahr•<u>zeen</u>•kah
shopping centre [BE] торговый
центр _tahr•goh•viy tsentr_
short adj **(height)** низкий
nees•keey
short-sighted [BE] близорукий
blee•zah•<u>roo</u>•keey
shorts шорты _shor•tih_
shoulder плечо _plee•<u>choh</u>_
shovel совок _sah•<u>vok</u>_
show v показывать
pah•<u>kah</u>•zih•vaht'
shower душ _doosh_
shut adj закрытый
zah•<u>krih</u>•tiy; v закрываться
zah•krih•<u>vah</u>•tsah
sick больной _bahl'•<u>noy</u>;_
side n **(of road)** сторона
stah•rah•<u>nah</u>
sightseeing tour обзорная
экскурсия _ahb•<u>zor</u>•nah•yah
eeks•<u>koor</u>•see•yah_
sign (road) знак _znahk_
silk шёлк _sholk_
silver серебро _see•ree•<u>broh</u>_
single (unmarried) холостой
khah•lah•<u>stoy</u>
single room одноместный
номер _ahd•nah•<u>myes</u>•niy
noh•meer_
single ticket [BE] билет в один
конец _bee•<u>lyet</u> v <u>ah</u>•deen
kah•<u>nyets</u>_
sink раковина
rah•kah•vee•nah
sit v сесть _syest'_
size размер _rahz•<u>myer</u>_
skates коньки _kahn'•<u>kee</u>_

ski boots лыжные ботинки
lizh•nih•yeh bah•teen•kee

skin кожа *koh•zhah*

skirt юбка *yoop•kah*

skis лыжи *lih•zhih*

sleep v спать *spaht'*

sleeping bag спальный мешок
spahl'•niy mee•shok

sleeping pill снотворное
snaht•vor•nah•yeh

sleeve рукав *roo•kahf*

slippers тапочки *tah•pach•kee*

slow adj медленный
myed•lee•niy

small (in size) маленький
mah•leen'•keey

smell n запах *zah•pahkh*

smoke v курить *koo•reet'*

smoking adj курящий
koo•ryah•shcheey

snack bar буфет *boo•fyet*

sneakers теннисные туфли
teh•nees•nih•ee toof•lee

snorkel n трубка *troop•kah*

snow снег *snyek*

soap мыло *mih•lah*

soccer футбол *food•bol*

socket розетка *rah•zyet•kah*

socks носки *nahs•kee*

sole (shoes) подошва
pah•dosh•vah

some какой-то *kah•koy tah*

someone кто-то *ktoh•tah*

something что-то *shtoh•tah*

sometimes иногда
ee•nahg•dah

soon скоро *skoh•rah*

soother [BE] соска *sos•kah*

sore throat ангина
ahn•gee•nah

souvenir сувенир *soo•vee•neer*

souvenir store магазин
сувениров *mah•gah•zeen
soo•vee•nee•rahf*

spa спа *spah*

space место *myes•tah*

spare (extra) лишний
leesh•neey

speak v говорить *gah•vah•reet'*

specialist специалист
spee•tsih•ah•leest

spell v называть по буквам
nah•zih•vaht' pah book•vahm

spend v тратить *trah•teet'*

spine позвоночник
pahz•vah•noch•neek

spoon ложка *losh•kah*

sport спорт *sport*

sports club спортклуб
sport•kloop

sporting goods
store спорттовары
spor•tah•vah•rih

sprain n растяжение
rahs•tee•zheh•nee•yeh

square adj квадратный
kvahd•raht•niy; n площадь
ploh•shchaht'

stadium стадион *stah•dee•on*

staff персонал *peer•sah•nahl*

stainless steel нержавеющая
сталь *nee•rzhah•vye•yoo•
shchah•yah stahl'*

stamp марка *mahr•kah*

stand v стоять *stah•yaht'*

start v (commence) начинать
nah•chee•naht'; (car)
заводить *zah•vah•deet'*

station вокзал *vahg•zahl*

stationery
канцелярские товары
*kahn•tsih•lyahr•skee•yeh
tah•vah•rih*

statue статуя *stah•too•yah*

stay v остаться *ah•stah•tsah*

sting укус *oo•koos*

stockings чулки *chool•kee*

stomach живот *zhih•vot*

stomachache болит живот
bah•leet zhih•vot

stop n (bus, etc.) остановка
ah•stah•nof•kah;
v останавливаться
ah•stah•nahv•lee•vah•tsah

store магазин *mah•gah•zeen*

store guide перечень отделов
pyeh•ree•cheen' ahd•dyeh•lahf

storm буря *boo•ryah*

stove плита *plee•tah*

strange странный *strah•niy*

stream ручей *roo•chey*

stroller прогулочная коляска
*prah•goo•lahch•nah•yah
kah•lyas•kah*

strong (potent) сильный
seel'•niy

student студент *stoo•dyent*

study v учиться *oo•chee•tsah*

stunning ошеломляющий
*ah•shih•lahm•lyah•
yoo•shcheey*

style стиль *steel'*

subtitled с субтитрами *s
soop•teet•rah•mee*

subway метро *meet•roh*

subway station станция метро
stahn•tsih•yah meet•roh

suggest предлагать
preed•lah•gaht'

suit костюм *kahs•tyoom*

sunbathe v загорать
zah•gah•raht'

sunburn солнечный ожёг
sol•neech•niy ah•zhok

sunglasses солнечные очки
sol•neech•nih•ee ahch•kee

sunny солнечно *sol•nyech•nah*

sunstroke солнечный удар
sol•neech•niy oo•dahr

superb превосходный
pree•vahs•khod•niy

supermarket универсам
oo•nee•veer•sahm

supervision присмотр
pree•smotr

supplement доплата
dah•plah•tah
surfboard доска для серфинга
dahs•kah dlyah ser•feen•gah
surname фамилия
fah•mee•lee•yah
suspicious подозрительный
pah•dah•zree•teel´•niy
sweater пуловер *poo•loh•veer*
sweatshirt байка *bie•kah*
swelling опухоль *oh•poo•khahl´*
swim *v* плавать *plah•vaht´*
swimming плавание
plah•vah•nee•yeh
swimming pool бассейн
bah•seyn
swimming trunks плавки
plahf•kee
swimsuit купальник
koo•pahl´•neek
symptoms симптомы
seemp•toh•mih
synagogue синагога
see•nah•goh•gah
synthetic синтетический
seen•teh•tee•chees•keey

T

T-shirt майка *mie•kah*
table столик *stoh•leek*
take (carry) нести *nyes•tee;*
(medication) принимать
pree•nee•maht´, **(time)**
занимать *zah•nee•maht´*
talk *v* разговаривать
rahz•gah•vah•ree•vaht´
tall высокий *vih•soh•keey*
tampon тампон *tahm•pon*
tan загар *zah•gahr*
taxi такси *tahk•see*
taxi rank [BE] стоянка такси
stah•yahn•kah tahk•see
taxi stand стоянка такси
stah•yahn•kah tahk•see
team команда *kah•mahn•dah*

teaspoon чайная ложка
chie•nah•yah losh•kah
teddy bear мишка *meesh•kah*
telephone *n* телефон
tee•lee•fon
telephone bill счёт за телефон
shchot zah tee•lee•fon
telephone booth
телефон-автомат
tee•lee•fon•ahf•tah•maht
telephone call телефонный
звонок *tee•lee•foh•niy
zvah•nok*
telephone directory
телефонный справочник
*tee•lee•foh•niy
sprah•vahch•neek*
telephone number номер
телефона *noh•meer
tee•lee•foh•nah*
tell *v* рассказывать
rahs•kah•zih•vaht´
temperature (body)
температура
teem•pee•rah•too•rah
tennis теннис *teh•nees*
tennis court теннисный корт
teh•nees•niy kort
tent палатка *pah•laht•kah*
tent pegs колышки
koh•lihsh•kee
tent pole шест *shest*
terminal (bus) (авто) вокзал
[aht•tah] vahg•zahl
terrible ужасный *ooh•zhahs•niy*
theater театр *tee•ahtr*
theft кража *krah•zhah*
then затем *zah•tyem*
there там *tahm*
thermometer термометр
teer•moh•meetr
thermos термос *ter•mahs*
thick толстый *tols•tiy*
thief вор *vor*
thigh бедро *beed•roh*

thin тонкий *ton´•keey*
think думать *doo•maht´*
throat горло *gor•lah*
through через *chyeh•rees*
thumb большой палец
bahl´•shoy pah•leets
ticket билет *bee•lyet*
ticket office билетные кассы
bee•lyet•nih•yeh kah•sih
tie галстук *gahls•took*
tight (loose) тесно *tyehs•niy*
tights колготки *kahl•got•kee*
time время *vryeh•myah*
timetable [BE] расписание
rahs•pee•sah•nee•yeh
tin [BE] банка *bahn•kah*
tin opener [BE] консервный
нож *kahn•serv•niy nosh*
tire *n* шина *shih•nah*
tired усталый *oos•tah•liy*
tissue бумажная салфетка
*boo•mazh•nah•yah
salh•fyet•kah*
to (place) в *v*
tobacco табак *tah•bahk*
toe палец ноги *pah•leets nah•gee*
together вместе *vmyes•tee*
toilet [BE] туалет *too•ah•lyet*
toilet paper туалетная бумага
*too•ah•lyet•nah•yah
boo•mah•gah*
tongue язык *yah•zihk*
too слишком *sleesh•kahm*
tooth зуб *zoop*
toothache зубная боль
zoob•nah•yah bol´
toothbrush зубная щётка
zoob•nah•yah shchot•kah
toothpaste зубная паста
zoob•nah•yah pahs•tah
top крышка *krihsh•kah*
tour экскурсия
eeks•koor•see•yah
tour guide экскурсовод
eeks•koor•sah•vot

tourist турист *too•reest*
tourist office
туристическое бюро
too•rees•tee•chees•kah•yeh byoo•roh
tow truck буксир *book•seer*
tow *v* отбуксировать
aht•book•see•rah•vaht'
towel полотенце
pah•lah•tyen•tseh
tower башня *bahsh•nyah*
town город *goh•raht*
town hall горсовет *gor•sah•vyet*
toy игрушка *eeg•roosh•kah*
track платформа *plaht•for•mah*
traditional традиционный
trah•dee•tsih•oh•niy
traffic дорожное движение
dah•rozh•nah•yeh dvee•zheh•nee•yeh
traffic jam пробка *prop•kah*
traffic lights светофор
svee•tah•for
trail трасса *trah•sah*
trailer трейлер *trey•leer*
train поезд *poh•eest*
train station вокзал *vahg•zahl*
tram трамвай *trahm•vie*
transit *n* проездом
prah•yez•dahm
translate *v* переводить
pee•ree•vah•deet'
translation перевод
pee•ree•vot
translator переводчик
pee•ree•vot•cheek
trash мусор *moo•sahr*
trash can мусорный бак
moo•sahr•niy bahk
travel agency бюро
путешествий *byoo•roh poo•tee•shest•veey*
travel sickness [BE] морская
болезнь *mahr•skah•yah bah•lyezn'*

traveler's check дорожный чек
dah•rozh•niy chehk
tray поднос *pahd•nos*
tree дерево *dyeh•ree•vah*
trim (hair) постричь *pah•streech*
trip (journey) поездка
pah•yest•kah
trolley [BE] тележка
tee•lyesh•kah
trousers [BE] брюки *bryoo•kee*
true правда *prahv•dah*
tunnel туннель *too•nel'*
turn down (volume, heat)
уменьшать *oo•meen'•shaht'*
turn off выключать
vih•klyoo•chaht'
turn on включать *fklyoo•chaht'*
turn up (volume, heat) увеличивать
oo•vee•lee•chee•vaht'
turning поворот *pah•vah•rot*
TV телевизор *teh•leh•vee•zahr*
typical типичный *tee•peech•niy*

U

ugly некрасивый
nee•krah•see•viy
ulcer язва *yahz•vah*
umbrella зонт *zont*
uncle дядя *dyah•dyah*
unconscious без сознания *byes
sahz•nah•nee•yah*
under под *paht*
underground [BE] метро
meet•roh
underground station [BE]
станция метро *stahn•tsih•yah meet•roh*
understand понимать
pah•nee•maht'
uneven (ground) неровный
nee•rov•niy
unfortunately к сожалению *k
sah•zhih•lyeh•nee•yoo*
uniform форма *for•mah*

unit (for phonecard, etc.)
единица *ee•dee•nee•tsah*
unleaded (gas) без свинца *bees
sveen•tsah*
unlock отпирать *aht•pee•raht'*
unpleasant неприятный
nee•pree•yaht•niy
upper (berth) верхний
vyerkh•neey
urgent срочно *sroch•nah*
urine моча *mah•chah*
use *v* пользоваться
pol'•zah•vah•tsah

V

vacant свободный *svah•bod•niy*
vacation отпуск *oht•poosk*
vacuum cleaner пылесос
pih•lee•sos
vaginal infection
вагинальная инфекция
*vah•gee•nahl'•nah•yah
een•fyek•tsih•yah*
valid действителен
deey•stvee•tee•len
valley долина *dah•lee•nah*
valuable ценность *tseh•niy*
value стоимость *stoh•ee•mahst'*
VAT [BE] НДС *en deh es*
vegetarian вегетарианец
vee•gee•tah•rah•ah•neets
vein вена *vyeh•nah*
very очень *oh•cheen'*
village деревня *dee•ryev•nyah*
visa виза *vee•zah*
visit *n* визит *vee•zeet;* *v*
посещать *pah•see•shchaht'*
visiting hours часы посещений
chee•sih pah•see•shcheh•neey
vitamins витамины
vee•tah•mee•nih
volleyball волейбол *vah•leey•bol*
voltage напряжение
nah•pree•zheh•nee•yeh
vomit тошнить *tahsh•neet'*

W

wait ждать *zhdaht'*
waiter официант
ah•fee•tsih•ahnt
waiting room зал ожидания
zahl ah•zhih•dah•nee•yah
wake (someone) разбудить
rahz•boo•deet'
walk v идти *eet•tee*
walking route пешеходный
маршрут *pee•shih•khod'niy
mahrsh•root*
wallet кошелёк *kah•shih•lyohk*
want хотеть *khah•tet'*
war memorial мемориал
mee•mah•ree•ahl
ward (hospital) палата
pah•lah•tah
warm тёплый *tyop•liy*
washing machine стиральная
машина *stee•rahl'•nah•yah
mah•shih•nah*
watch часы *chah•sih*
water вода *vah•dah*
water skis водные лыжи
vod•nih•yeh lih•zhee
waterfall водопад *vah•dah•paht*
waterproof

водонепроницаемый *voh•dah
•nee•prah•nee•tsah•ee•miy*
wave волна *vahl•nah*
wear v одевать *ah•dee•vaht'*
weather погода *pah•goh•dah*
weather forecast прогноз
погоды *prahg•nos
pah•goh•dih*
wedding свадьба *svahd'•bah*
week неделя *nee•deh•lyah*
weekend выходные
vih•khahd•nih•yeh
weigh вес *ves*
wheelchair инвалидное кресло
*een•vah•leed•nah•yeh
kryes•lah*
wide широкий *shih•roh•keey*
wife жена *zhih•nah*
windbreaker ветровка
veet•rof•kah
window окно *ahk•noh*
window seat место у окна
myes•tah oo ahk•nah
windscreen ветровое стекло
vee•trah•voh•yeh steek•loh
windsurfer виндсерфер
veend•syer•fyer
windy ветер *vyeh•teer*

wireless internet беспроводной
интернет *bees•prah•vahd•noy
een•ter•net*
with с *s*
withdraw снимать *snee•maht'*
without без *bes*
wood лес *lyes*
wool шерсть *sherst'*
work v работать *rah•boh•taht'*
wound п рана *rah•nah*
wrong неправильный
nee•prah•veel'•niy

X

X-ray рентген *reen•gyen*

Y

yacht яхта *yahkh•tah*
yellow жёлтый *zhol•tiy*
young молодой *mah•lah•doy*
youth hostel общежитие
ahp•shchee•zhih•tee•yeh

Z

zebra crossing переход
pee•ree•khot
zipper молния *mol•nee•yah*
zoo зоопарк *zah•oh•pahrk*

A

аванс *ah•vahns* deposit
аварийный выход *ah•vah•reey•
niy vih•khaht* emergency exit
автобус *ahf•toh•boos* bus
автобусная остановка
*ahf•toh•boos•nah•yah
ahs•tah•nof•kah* bus stop
автобусная станция
*ahf•toh•boos•nah•yah
stahn•tsih•yah* bus station

автовокзал *ahf•tah vahg•zahl*
terminal (bus)
автостоянка
ahf•tah•stah•yahn•kah parking lot [car park BE]
адаптер *ah•dahp•ter* adapter
адвокат *ahd•vah•kaht* lawyer
адрес *ahd•dres* address
адрес электронной почты
*ah•drees ee•leek•tron•nie
poch•tih* e-mail address

аккумулятор
ah•kah•moo•lyah•tahr battery
аллергия *ah•leer•gee•yah*
allergy
американский *ah•mee•ree•
kahn•skeey adj* American
ангина *ahn•gee•nah* sore throat
английский *ahn•gleey•skeey*
English
антибиотики *ahn•tee•bee•
oh•tee•kee* antibiotics

антикварный
ahn•tee•kvahr•niy antique

антисептик *ahn•tee•sep•teek*
antiseptic

аппендикс *ah•pyen•deeks*
appendix

аптека *ahp•tyeh•kah* pharmacy
[chemist BE]

аспирин *ah•spee•reen* aspirin

астматик *ahst•mah•teek* n
asthmatic

аэропорт *ah•eh•rah•port* airport

Б

багаж *bah•gahsh* luggage
[baggage BE]

багажная квитанция *bah•gahzh•nah•yah kvee•tahn•tsih•yah* baggage check

багажная тележка
bah•gahzh•nah•yah tee•lyesh•kah luggage cart
[trolley BE]

байка *bie•kah* sweatshirt

балет *bah•lyet* ballet

балкон *bahl•kon* balcony

банк *bahnk* bank

банка *bahn•kah* jar; can [tin BE]

банкомат *bahn•kah•maht* ATM

бар *bahr* bar (hotel, etc.)

баскетбол *bahs•keet•bol*
basketball

бассейн *bah•seyn* swimming
pool

башня *bahsh•nyah* tower

бега *bee•gah* horse racing

бедро *beed•roh* thigh

без *byez* without

без сознания *byes sah•znah•nee•yah* unconscious

безопасность
bee•zah•pahs•nahst' safety

безопасный *bee•zah•pahs•niy adj* safe

бензин *been•zeen* gas [petrol
BE]

беременна *bee•ryeh•mee•nah*
pregnant

беспокоить *bees•pah•koh•eet'*
disturb

беспроводной интернет
bees•prah•vahd•noy een•ter•net wireless internet

бессонница *bees•soh•nee•tsah*
insomnia

библиотека
bee•blee•ah•tyeh•kah library

бизнес *beez•nees* business

бикини *bee•kee•nee* bikini

билет *bee•lyet* ticket

билет в один конец *bee•lyet
v ah•deen kah•nyets* one-way
[single BE] ticket

билет туда и обратно *bee•lyet
too•dah ee ahb•raht•nah*
round-trip [return BE] ticket

билетная касса
bee•lyet•nah•yah kah•sah
ticket office

бинокль *bee•noh•kahl'*
binoculars

близорукий *blee•zah•roo•keey*
near-sighted [short-sighted
BE]

блузка *bloos•kah* blouse

болеть *bah•lyet'* v hurt

болеутоляющее *boh•lee•oo•tah•lyah•yoo•shchee•yeh*
painkiller

боль *bol'* pain

больница *bahl'•nee•tsah*
hospital

большой *bahl'•shoy* big

большой палец *bahl'•shoy
pah•leets* thumb

ботанический сад
bah•tah•nee•chees•keey saht
botanical garden

бояться *bah•yah•tsah* frightened

браслет *brahs•lyet* bracelet

брат *braht* brother

брильянт *breel'•yahnt* diamond

британский *bree•tahn•skeey*
British

бритва *breet•vah* razor

бронхит *brahn•kheet* bronchitis

брошь *brosh* brooch

брошюра *brah•shoo•rah*
brochure

брюки *bryoo•kee* pants
[trousers BE]

будильник *boo•deel'•neek*
alarm clock

буксир *book•seer* tow truck

буксировать
book•see•rah•vaht' tow

булавка *boo•lahf•kah* safety pin

булочная *boo•lahch•nah•yah*
bakery

бумага *boo•mah•gah* paper

бумажная салфетка
*boo•mahzh•nah•yah
sahl•fyet•kah* tissue

буря *boo•ryah* storm

буфет *boo•fyet* snack bar

бухгалтер *boo•gahl•teer*
accountant

быстрый *bihs•triy* quick

быть *biht'* be

бюро находок *byoo•roh
nah•khoh•dahk* lost-and-found
[lost property office BE]

бюстгальтер *byoost•gahl•ter*
bra

В

вагинальная инфекция
*vah•gee•nahl'•nah•yah
een•fyek•tsih•yah* vaginal
infection

вагон *vah•gon* car [coach BE]
(train)

вагон-ресторан *vah•gon
rees•tah•rahn* dining car

валюта vah•_lyoo_•tah currency
вантуз vahn•toos plunger
вата vah•tah cotton
вегетарианец vee•gee•tah•
ree•_ah_•neets vegetarian
ведро veed•roh bucket
Великобритания
vee•lee•kah•bree•
tah•nee•yah Great Britain
великолепный
vee•lee•kah•_lyep_•niy
magnificent
велосипед vee•lah•see•pyet
bicycle
велосипедный маршрут
•vee•lah•see•_pyed_•niy
mahrsh•_root_ cycle route
велоспорт vyeh•lah•_sport_
cycling
вена vyeh•nah vein
вентилятор veen•tee•lyah•tahr
fan (air)
веревка vee•_ryof_•kah rope
верхний _vyerkh_•neey upper
вес vyes weight
веселье vee•_syel_•yeh fun
ветер _vyeh_•teer wind
ветровка veet•_rof_•kah
windbreaker
ветровое стекло
vee•trah•_vo_•yeh steek•_loh_
windscreen
вечеринка vee•chee•_reen_•kah
party (social)
вешалка vye•shahl•kah peg
взлом vzlom break-in
взрослый vzros•liy adult
взять напрокат vzyat'
nah•prah•_kaht_ v rent (hire BE)
видеть vee•deet' see
виза vee•zah visa
визит vee•_zeet_ n visit
вилка veel•kah fork
виндсерфер veend•_syer_•fyer
windsurfer

винный магазин vee•niy
mah•gah•_zeen_ liquor store
[off-license BE]
витамины vee•tah•_mee_•nih
vitamins
витрина vee•_tree_•nah window
(in store)
владелец vlah•_dyeh_•leets
owner
вместе _vmyes_•tee together
внутри vnoo•_tree_ inside
вовремя _voh_•vryeh•myah
on time
вода vah•_dah_ n water
водитель vah•_dee_•teel' driver
водительские права
vah•_dee_•teel'•skee•yeh
prah•vah driver's license
водная экскурсия vod•nah•yah
eks•_koor_•see•yah boat trip
водные лыжи vod•nih•yeh
lih•zhih water skis
водонепроницаемый voh•da
h•nee•prah•nee•_tsah_•ee•m
y waterproof
водопад vah•dah•_paht_
water fall
воздух voz•dookh air
возраст voz•rahst n age
вокзал vahg•_zahl_ train [railway
BE] station
волдырь vahl•_dihr'_ blister
волейбол vah•leey•_bol_
volleyball
волна vahl•_nah_ n wave
волосы voh•lah•sih hair
вор vor thief
воспаление
vahs•pah•_lyeh_•nee•yeh
inflammation
врач vrahch doctor
время vryeh•myah time
все fsyoh all
все еще vsyoh ee•_shchoh_ still
всегда fseeg•dah always

вставлять fstahv•_lyat'_ v insert
встречаться fstree•_chah_•tsah
meet
второй ftah•_roy_ second
вход в систему fkhot f
sees•_tyeh_•moo n login
входная плата fkhahd•_nah_•yah
plah•tah entrance fee
въездная виза vyezd•_nah_•yah
vee•zah entry visa
вывихнуть vih•_veekh_•noot'
v twist
выезжать vih•eezh•_zhaht'_
check-out (hotel)
вызывать _vih_•zih•vaht' v call
(the police)
выписывать vih•_pee_•sih•vaht'
prescribe
высокий vih•_soh_•keey high
высокий vih•_soh_•keey tall
высокое давление
vih•soh•kah•yeh dahv•_lyeh_•
nee•yeh high blood pressure
выход vih•khahd n exit
выходные vih•khahd•_nih_•yeh
weekend

Г

гавань gah•vahn' harbor
газета gah•_zyeh_•tah newspaper
газетный киоск gah•_zyet_•niy
kee•osk newsstand
галлон gah•_lon_ gallon
галстук gahls•took tie
гандикап gahn•dee•_kahp_
handicap (golf)
гараж gah•_rahsh_ garage
гарантия gah•_rahn_•tee•yah
guarantee
гардероб gahr•dee•_rop_
coatcheck
гигиенические салфетки
gee•gee•ee•_nee_•chees•kee•
yeh sahl•_fyet_•kee sanitary
napkins [pads BE]

гид *geet* guide (tour)
гинеколог *gee•nee•koh•lahk* gynecologist
гитара *gee•tah•rah* guitar
главный *glahv•niy* main
глаз *glahs* eye
глубокий *gloo•boh•keey* deep
глухой *gloo•khoy* deaf
говорить *gah•vah•reet'* speak
голова *gah•lah•vah* head
головная боль
gah•lahv•nah•yah bol' headache
голодный *gah•lod•niy* hungry
гололёд *gah•lah•lyot* icy
гольф *gol'f* golf
гора *gah•rah* mountain
горло *gor•lah* throat
город *goh•raht* town
горсовет *gor•sah•vyet* town hall
горячий *gah•rya•cheey* hot
гостиная *gahs•tee•nah•yah* living room
гостиница *gahs•tee•nee•tsah* hotel
готовить *gah•toh•veet'* prepare
готовый *gah•toh•viy* ready
грабёж *grah•byosh* robbery
градус *grah•doos* degree (temperature)
грамм *grahm* gram
графин *grah•feen* carafe
грипп *greep* flu
громче *grom•chee* louder
грудная клетка *grood•nah•yah klyet•kah* chest (body)
грудь *groot'* breast
группа *groo•pah* group
группа крови *groo•pah kroh•vee* blood group
грязный *gryahz•niy* dirty
губа *goo•bah* lip
губная памада *goob•nah•yah pah•mah•dah* lipstick

Д

давать *dah•vaht'* give
далеко *dah•lee•koh* far
дальнозоркий *dahl'•nah•zor•keey* far-sighted [long-sighted BE]
дать взаймы *daht' vzie•mih* lend
дача *dah•chah* summer cottage
дверь *dvyer'* door
движение *dah•rozh•nah•yeh dvee•zheh•nee•yeh* traffic
дворец *dvah•ryets* palace
двухместный *dvookh•myes•niy* double
девочка *dyeh•vahch•kah* girl
дезодорант *dee•zah•dah•rahnt* deodorant
действителен *deey•stvee•tee•lyen* valid
делать ставку *dyeh•laht' stahf•koo* place a bet
день *dyen'* day
день рождения *dyen' rahzh•dyeh•nee•yah* birthday
деньги *dyen'•gee* money
деревня *dee•ryev•nyah* village
дерево *dyeh•ree•vah* tree
десна *dees•nah* gum
детальный счёт *dee•tahl'•niy shchot* itemized bill
дети *dyeh•tee* children
детская площадка *dyets•kah•yah plah•shchaht'•kah* playground
детское сиденье *dyets•kah•yeh see•dyen'•yeh* child seat (in car)
дешевле *dee•shev•lee* cheaper
дешёвый *dee•shoh•viy* cheap
джаз *dzhahs* jazz
джинсовый *dzhihn•soh•viy adj* denim
джинсы *dzhihn•sih* jeans
диабет *dee•ah•byet* diabetes

диабетик *dee•ah•byeh•teek* diabetic (person)
диагноз *dee•ahg•nahs* diagnosis
диета *dee•yeh•tah n* diet
дизельное топливо *dee•zeel'•nah•yeh top•lee•vah* diesel
директор *dee•ryek•tahr* director (of company)
дирижёр *dee•ree•zhor* conductor (orchestra)
длина *dlee•nah* length
длинный *dlee•niy* long
дневное представление *dneev•noh•yeh preet•stahv•lyeh•nee•yeh* matinée
до *dah* until
добавочный номер *dah•bah•vahch•niy noh•meer* extension
добираться *dah•bee•rah•tsah* get (to destination)
дождь *doshch n* rain
долина *dah•lee•nah* valley
дом *dom* house
допуск *doh•poosk n* access
дорога *dah•roh•gah* road
дорогой *dah•rah•goy* expensive
дорожная пробка *dah•rozh•nah•yah prop•kah* traffic jam
дорожный чек *dah•rozh•niy chehk* traveler's check [cheques BE]
доска для серфинга *dahs•kah dlyah ser•feen•gah* surfboard
доставлять *dah•stahv•lyat'* deliver
достаточно *dah•stah•tahch•nah* enough
дрова *drah•vah* firewood
друг *drook* friend
другие *droo•gee•yeh* others

другой droo•_goy_ other
дружеский droo•_zhees_•keey friendly
дублирован doob•_lee_•rah•vahn dubbed
думать _doo_•maht´ think
духовка doo•_khof_•kah oven
душ doosh shower
дырка _dihr_•kah hole (in clothes)
дышать dih•_shaht´_ breathe
дюжина _dyoo_•zhih•nah dozen
дядя _dyah_•dyah uncle

Е

Европейский союз yev•rah•_pey_•skeey sah•_yoos_ European Union (EU)
ежедневно ee•zhee•_dnyev_•nah daily
ерунда ee•_roon_•dah nonsense
есть yest´ eat
ехать _yeh_•khaht´ drive
ещё ee•_shchoh_ extra (additional)

Ж

жалоба _zhah_•lah•bah complaint
жар zhahr fever
ждать zhdaht´ wait
жёлтый _zhol_•tiy yellow
жемчуг zhem•chook pearl
жена zhih•nah wife
женат zhih•naht married (man)
живописный маршрут zhih•vah•_pees_•niy mahrsh•root scenic route
живот zhih•vot stomach
животное zhi•_vot_•nah•yeh animal
журнал zhoor•nahl magazine

З

забирать zah•bee•_raht´_ collect
заблокирован zah•blah•_kee_•rah•vahn blocked

заболевание сердца zah•bah•lee•_vah_•nee•yeh _syer_•tsah heart condition
заболеть zah•bah•_lyet´_ get sick (ill BE)
забывать zah•bih•_vaht´_ forget
загар zah•_gahr_ tan
загорать zah•gah•_raht´_ sunbathe
заграницей zah•grah•_nee_•tsey abroad
задержка zah•_dyersh_•kah n delay
зажигалка zah•zhih•_gahl_•kah lighter (cigarette)
заказывать zah•_kah_•zih•vaht´ v order
законный zah•_kon_•niy legal
закрываться zah•krih•_vah_•tsah v close (store, etc.)
закрытый zah•_krih_•tiy adj shut
закрытый бассейн zah•_krih_•tiy bah•_seyn_ indoor pool
зал вылета zahl _vih_•lee•tah departure lounge
зал ожидания zahl ah•zhih•_dah_•nee•yah waiting room
замок _zah_•mahk castle
замок zah•_mok_ n lock
замужем _zah_•moo•zhihm married (woman)
занят _zah_•nyaht busy
занятый _zah_•nee•tiy occupied
запах _zah_•pahkh smell
заповедник zah•pah•_vyed_•neek nature reserve
заправочная станция zah•_prah_•vahch•nah•yah _stahn_•tsih•yah gas station
затем zah•_tyem_ then (time)
захватывающий zah•_khvah_•tih•vah•yoo•shcheey breathtaking

заштопать zah•_shtoh_•paht´ patch
звонить zvah•_neet´_ v call (phone)
здание _zdah_•nee•yeh building
здесь zdyes´ here
зелёный zee•_lyo_•niy green
зеркало zyer•_kah_•lah mirror
знак znahk sign (road)
значить zah•_cheet´_ v mean
золото zoh•lah•tah gold
зонт zont umbrella
зоопарк zah•ah•_pahrk_ n zoo
зуб zoop tooth
зубная боль zoob•_nah_•yah bol´ tooth-ache
зубная паста zoob•_nah_•yah _pahs_•tah toothpaste
зубная щётка zoob•_nah_•yah _shchot_•kah toothbrush
зубной врач zoob•noy vrahch dentist

И

игра eeg•_rah_ game
играть eeg•_raht´_ v play (games, etc.)
игрушка eeg•_roosh_•kah n toy
идти за покупками eet•tee zah pah•_koop_•kah•mee go shopping
идти пешком eet•tee peesh•_kom_ v walk
из-за eez•zah because of
измерение eez•mee•_ryeh_•nee•yeh measurement
измерить eez•_myeh_•reet´ v measure
изнасилование eez•nah•_see_•lah•vah•nee•yeh n rape
изумруд ee•zoom•_root_ emerald
изучать ee•zoo•_chaht´_ learn (language)
имя ee•myah name (first name)

инвалид _een•vah•<u>leet</u>_ n handicapped [disabled BE]

инвалидное кресло _een•vah•<u>leed</u>•nah•yeh <u>kryes</u>•lah_ wheelchair

иногда _ee•nahg•<u>dah</u>_ sometimes

иностранная валюта _ee•nah•<u>strah</u>•nah•yah vah•<u>lyoo</u>•tah_ foreign currency

инструкция _een•<u>strook</u>•tsih•yah_ instructions

инсулин _een•soo•<u>leen</u>_ insulin

интересный _een•tee•<u>ryes</u>•niy_ interesting

интернет _een•ter•<u>net</u>_ internet

интернет-кафе _een•ter•<u>net</u> kah•<u>feh</u>_ internet cafe

инфекция _een•<u>fyek</u>•tsih•yah_ infection

информация _een•fahr•<u>mah</u>•tsih•yah_ information

ипподром _ee•pah•<u>drom</u>_ racetrack

исполнять _ees•pahl•<u>nyaht'</u>_ perform

К

к сожалению _k sah•zhih•<u>lyeh</u>•nee•yoo_ unfortunately

к счастью _k <u>shchahst'</u>•yoo_ fortunately

каждый _<u>kahzh</u>•diy_ every

казино _kah•zee•<u>noh</u>_ casino

какой-либо _kah•<u>koy</u>•lee•bah_ any

какой-то _kah•<u>koy</u> tah_ some

календарь _kah•leen•<u>dahr'</u>_ calendar

камера хранения _<u>kah</u>•mee•rah khrah•<u>nyeh</u>•nee•yah_ luggage locker

канцелярские товары _kahn•tsih•<u>lyahr</u>•skee•yeh tah•<u>vah</u>•rih_ stationery

карандаш _kah•rahn•<u>dahsh</u>_ pencil

карта _<u>kahr</u>•tah_ map

карта дорог _<u>kahr</u>•tah dah•<u>rok</u>_ road map

картина _kahr•<u>tee</u>•nah_ painting

картинная галерея _kahr•<u>teen</u>•nah•yah gah•lee•<u>ryeh</u>•yah_ art gallery

карты _<u>kahr</u>•tih_ cards

кассета _kah•<u>syeh</u>•tah_ cassette

кассир _kah•<u>seer</u>_ cashier

кастрюля _kahs•<u>tryoo</u>•lyah_ saucepan

качество _<u>kah</u>•chees•tvah_ quality

кашель _<u>kah</u>•shihl'_ n cough

кашлять _<u>kahsh</u>•lyaht'_ v cough

каюта _kah•<u>yoo</u>•tah_ cabin

квадратный _kvahd•<u>raht</u>•niy_ adj square

квартира _kvahr•<u>tee</u>•rah_ apartment [flat BE]

кемпинг _<u>kyem</u>•peenk_ camping

керамика _kee•<u>rah</u>•mee•kah_ pottery

километраж _kee•lah•mee•<u>trahsh</u>_ mileage

кинотеатр _kee•nah•tee•<u>ahtr</u>_ movie theater [cinema BE]

кишечник _kee•<u>shech</u>•neek_ bowel

класс _klahs_ class (type of seat, etc.)

ключ _klyooch_ key

клюшка _<u>klyoosh</u>•kah_ club (golf)

книга _<u>knee</u>•gah_ book

книжный магазин _<u>kneezh</u>•niy mah•gah•<u>zeen</u>_ bookstore

кнопка _<u>knop</u>•kah_ button

ковер _kah•<u>vyor</u>_ carpet (rug)

код _kot_ area code

кожа _<u>koh</u>•zhah_ leather (material); skin (body)

колготки _kahl•<u>got</u>•kee_ tights

колено _kah•<u>lyeh</u>•nah_ knee

кольцо _kahl•<u>tsoh</u>_ n ring

команда _kah•<u>mahn</u>•dah_ team

командировка _kah•mahn•dee•<u>rof</u>•kah_ business trip

комариный укус _kah•mah•<u>ree</u>•niy oo•<u>koos</u>_ mosquito bite

комиссионный сбор _kah•mee•see•<u>oh</u>•niy zbor_ n commission

комната _<u>kom</u>•nah•tah_ room (house)

компакт-диск _kahm•<u>pahkt</u> deesk_ CD

компания _kahm•<u>pah</u>•nee•yah_ company (companionship)

конверт _kahn•<u>vyert</u>_ envelope

кондитерская _kahn•<u>dee</u>•teer•skah•yah_ pastry store

кондиционер _kahn•dee•tsih•ah•<u>nyer</u>_ conditioner

консервный нож _kahn•<u>syerv</u>•niy nosh_ can [tin BE] opener

консульство _<u>kon</u>•sool'•stvah_ consulate

консультироваться _kahn•sool'•<u>tee</u>•rah•vah•tsah_ consult

контактные линзы _kahn•<u>tahkt</u>•nih•yeh leen•zih_ contact lenses

концерт _kahn•<u>tsert</u>_ concert

концертный зал _kahn•<u>tsert</u>•niy zahl_ concert hall

кончаться _kahn•<u>chah</u>•tsah_ v end

коньки _kahn'•<u>kee</u>_ skates

копия _koh•pee•yah_ copy
корабль _kah•rahbl'_ ship
корзина _kahr•zee•nah_ basket
кормить _kahr•meet'_ feed
коронка _kah•ron•kah_ cap (dental)
косметика _kahs•myeh•tee•kah_ cosmetics
костыли _kahs•tih•lee_ crutches
кость _kost'_ bone
костюм _kahs•tyoom_ n suit
кошелёк _kah•shih•lyok_ wallet
кошерный _kah•sher•niy_ kosher
кража _krah•zhah_ theft
крайний случай _krie•neey sloo•chie_ emergency
кран _krahn_ faucet [tap BE]
красивый _krah•see•viy_ beautiful
кредитная карточка _kree•deet•nah•yah kahr•tahch•kah_ credit card
крем для загара _kryem dlyah zah•gah•rah_ sun-tan cream
кровать _krah•vaht'_ bed
кровотечение _krah•vah•tee•cheh•nee•yeh_ bleeding
кровь _krof'_ blood
кровяное давление _krah•vee•noh•yeh dahv•lyel•nee•yeh_ blood pressure
кроме _kroh•mee_ except
круглый _kroog•liy_ round
кружево _kroo•zhih•vah_ lace
кружка _kroosh•kah_ n mug
круиз _kroo•ees_ cruise
крыша _krih•shah_ roof (house, car)
ксерокс _ksyeh•rahks_ photocopier
кто-нибудь _ktoh•nee•boot'_ anyone
кто-то _ktoh•tah_ someone

кукла _kook•lah_ doll
кукольный театр _koo•kahl'•niy tee•ahtr_ puppet show
купальник _koo•pahl'•neek_ swimsuit
купе _koo•peh_ compartment (train)
курить _koo•reet'_ v smoke
курс обмена _koors ahb•myeh•nah_ exchange rate
курящий _koo•ryah•shcheey_ adj smoking
кусочек _koo•soh•cheek_ piece

Л

лавина _lah•vee•nah_ avalanche
лазерный проигрыватель _lah•zeer•niy prah•eeg•rih•vah•teel'_ CD-player
лак для волос _lahk dlyah vah•los_ hair spray
лампа _lahm•pah_ lamp
лампочка _lahm•pahch•kah_ light bulb
лёгкий _lyokh•keey_ light (opp. heavy); easy
лёгкое _lyokh•kah•yeh_ lung
лезвие _lyez•vee•yeh_ razor blade
лекарство _lee•kahr•stvah_ medication
лес _lyes_ forest
линия _lee•nee•yah_ line (metro)
лифт _leeft_ elevator [lift BE]
лицо _lee•tsoh_ face
лишний _leesh•neey_ spare (extra)
лодка _lot•kah_ boat
ложка _losh•kah_ spoon
лосьон после бритья _lahs'•yon pos•lee breet'•yah_ after-shave
лошадь _loh•shahd'_ horse
лучше _looch•sheh_ better
лыжи _lih•zhih_ skis
лыжные ботинки _lizh•nih•yeh bah•teen•kee_ ski boots

любезный _lyoo•byez•niy_ kind (pleasant)
любимый _lyoo•bee•miy_ favorite
любить _lyoo•beet'_ v love
люди _lyoo•dee_ people

М

магазин _mah•gah•zeen_ store
майка _mie•kah_ T-shirt
макияж _mah•kee•yash_ n make-up
маленький _mah•leen'•keey_ little (small)
мало _mah•lah_ few; little
мальчик _mahl'•cheek_ boy
манеж _mah•nyesh_ playpen
маникюр _mah•nee•kyoor_ manicure
марка _mahr•kah_ stamp
маска _mahs•kah_ mask (diving)
массаж _mah•sahsh_ n massage
матрас _maht•rahs_ mattress
матрёшка _maht•ryosh•kah_ nesting doll
матч _mahch_ match (sport)
машина _mah•shih•nah_ car
мебель _myeh•beel'_ furniture
медленный _myed•lee•niy_ slow
медовый месяц _mee•doh•viy myeh•syats_ honeymoon
медсестра _myet•sees•trah_ nurse
медь _myet'_ copper
междугородний автобус _meezh•doo•gah•rod•niy ahf•to•boos_ coach (long-distance bus)
мелировать _mee•lee•rah•vaht'_ v highlight (hair)
мелкий _mel•keey_ shallow
мемориал _mee•mah•ree•ahl_ war memorial
менять _mee•nyaht'_ v change
местный _myes•niy_ local

местный наркоз _myes•niy_ _nahr•kos_ local anesthetic

место _myes•tah_ place (space)

место багажа _myes•tah_ _bah•gah•zhah_ piece of luggage

место назначения _myes•tah_ _nahz•nah•cheh•nee•yah_ destination

место у окна _myes•tah oo_ _ahk•nah_ window seat

место у прохода _myes•tah oo_ _prah•khoh•dah_ aisle seat

месяц _myeh•syahts_ month

металл _mee•tahl_ metal

метро _meet•roh_ subway [underground BE]

мечеть _mee•chet'_ mosque

мигрень _meeg•ryen'_ migraine

микроволновая печь _meek•rah•vahl•noh•vah•yah_ _pyech_ microwave

милиция _mee•lee•tsih•yah_ police

минута _mee•noo•tah_ minute

мобильный телефон _mah•beel'•niy tee•lee•fon_ cell [mobile BE] phone

мой _moy_ my

молния _mol•nee•yah_ zipper

молодой _mah•lah•doy_ young

монета _mah•nyeh•tah_ coin

море _moh•ryeh_ sea

мороз _mah•ros_ frost

морозильная камера _mah•rah•zeel'•nah•yah_ _kah•mee•rah_ freezer

морская болезнь _mahr•skah•yah bah•lyezn'_ motion [travel BE] sickness

мост _most_ bridge

моторка _mah•tor•kah_ motorboat

мотоцикл _mah•tah•tsihkl_ motorbike

моча _mah•chah_ urine

мочевой пузырь _mah•chee•voy_ _poo•zihr'_ bladder

моющее средство _moh•yoo•shchee•yeh_ _sryet•stvah_ detergent

муж _moosh_ husband

мужчина _moo•shchee•nah_ man (male)

музей _moo•zyey_ museum

музыка _moo•zih•kah_ music

мусор _moo•sahr_ trash [rubbish BE]

мусорный бак _moo•sahr•niy_ _bahk_ trash can [dustbin BE]

мы _mih_ we

мыло _mih•lah_ soap

мышца _mihsh•tsah_ muscle

мяч _myahch_ ball

Н

на открытом воздухе _nah_ _aht•krih•tahm voz•doo•khee_ outdoor

на пенсии _nah pyen•see•ee_ retired

на улице _nah oo•lee•tseh_ outside

называть по буквам _nah•zih•vaht' pah book•vahm_ v spell

наконец _nah•kah•nyets_ at last

наличные _nah•leech•nih•yeh_ n cash

нападение _nah•pah•dyeh•nee•yeh n_ attack

направление _nah•prahv•lyeh•nee•yeh_ direction

направлять _nah•prahv•lyaht'_ v direct

например _nah•pree•myer_ for example

напротив _nah•proh•teef_ opposite

напряжение _nah•pree•zheh•nee•yeh_ voltage

народная музыка _nah•rod•nah•yah moo•zih•kah_ folk music

народное искусство _nah•rod•nah•yeh_ _ees•koos•tvah_ folk art

насекомое _nah•see•koh•mah•yeh_ insect

насос _nah•sos_ n pump

настаивать _nah•stah•ee•vaht'_ insist

настоящий _nah•stah•yah•shcheey_ real (genuine)

национальность _nah•tsih•ah•nahl'•nahst'_ nationality

национальный _nah•tsih•ah•nahl'•niy_ national

начинать _nah•chee•naht'_ begin

начинаться _nah•chee•nah•tsah_ v start

НДС _en deh es_ sales tax [VAT BE]

невероятный _nee•vee•rah•yaht•niy_ incredible

невиновен _nee•vee•noh•veen_ innocent

неделя _nee•deh•lyah_ week

недоразумение _nee•dah•rah•zoo•myeh•nee•yeh_ misunderstanding

недорогой _nee•dah•rah•goy_ inexpensive

незаконный _nee•zah•kon•niy_ illegal

некрасивый _nee•krah•see•viy_ ugly

некурящий _nee•koo•ryah•shcheey adj_ non-smoking

немедленно _nee•myeh•dlee•nah_ immediately

неплохо *nee•ploh•khah* not bad
неправильный *nee•prah•veel´•niy* wrong
неприятный *nee•pree•yaht•niy* unpleasant
нерв *nyerf* nerve
нержавеющая сталь *nee•rzhah•vyeh•yoo•shchah•yah stahl´* stainless steel
неровный *nee•rov•niy* uneven (ground)
несложный *nyeh•slozh•niy* easy
несчастный случай *nee•shchahs•niy sloo•chie* accident
низкий *nees•kiy* short (height)
никогда *nee•kahg•dah* never
никто *nee•ktoh* no one
ничего *nee•chee•yoh* nothing
новый *noh•viy* new
нога *nah•gah* foot; leg
нож *nosh* knife
ножницы *nozh•nee•tsih* scissors
номер *noh•meer* number (telephone)
нормальный *nahr•mahl´•niy* normal
нос *nos* nose
носильщик *nah•seel´•shcheek* porter
носки *nahs•kee* socks
ночной *nahch•noy* all-night
ночью *noh•chyoo* at night
нравиться *nrah•vee•tsah* v enjoy
нырять *nih•ryat´* v dive

о

обед *ah•byet* lunch
обезболивающее *ah•beez•b oh•lee•vah•yoo•shchee•yeh* anaesthetic
обзорная экскурсия *ahb•zor•nah•yah eeks•koor•see•yah* sightseeing tour

облачно *ob•lahch•nah* cloudy
обмен валюты *ahb•myen vah•lyoo•tih* currency exchange office
обменивать *ahb•myeh•nee•vaht´* exchange
обогреватель *ah•bah•gree•vah•teel´* heater
обслуживание номеров *ahp•sloo•zhih•vah•nee•yeh nah•mee•rof* room service
обувной магазин *ah•boov•noy mah•gah•zeen* shoe store
общежитие *ahp•shchee•zhih•tee•yeh* youth hostel
обязательный *ah•bee•zah•teel´•niy* necessary
огнетушитель *ahg•nee•too•shih•teel´* fire extinguisher
ограбление *ah•grahb•lyeh•nee•yeh* mugging; robbery
одевать *ah•dee•vat´* put on; wear
одежда *ah•dyezh•dah* clothes
одеяло *ah•dee•yah•lah* blanket
один *ah•deen* alone
один раз *ah•deen rahs* once
одноместный номер *ahd•nah•myes•niy noh•meer* single room
одолжить *ah•dahl•zhit´* borrow
ожерелье *ah•zhih•ryel´•yeh* necklace
ожог *ah•zhok* n burn
озеро *oh•zee•rah* lake
окно *ahk•noh* window
около *oh•kah•lah* about (approximately); near
опаздывать *ah•pahz•dih•vaht´* be delayed
опасный *ah•pahs•niy* dangerous

опера *oh•pee•rah* opera
операция *ah•pee•rah´•tsih•yah* operation
описывать *ah•pee•sih•vaht´* describe
оплата *ah•plah•tah* payment
оправа *ah•prah•vah* n frame (glasses)
оптика *op•tee•kah* optician
оркестр *ahr•kyestr* orchestra
осмотр *ahs•motr* examination (medical)
основной *ahs•nahv•noy* essential
останавливаться *as•stah•nahv•lee•vah•tsah v* stop
остановка *ahs•tah•nof•kah n* stop (bus, etc.)
остаться *ah•stah•tsah v* stay
осторожный *ahs•tah•rozh•niy* careful
отбеливатель *aht•byeh•lee•vah•teel´* bleach
отвёртка *aht•vyort•kah* screwdriver
отвратительный *aht•vrah•tee•teel´•niy* revolting
отдавать в химчистку *aht•dah•vaht´ f kheem•cheest•koo v* dry clean
отдел *aht•dyel* department (in store)
отделение милиции *aht•dee•lyeh•nee•yeh mee•lee•tsih•ee* police station
отдельно *ahd•del´•nah* separately
отдыхать *aht•dih•khat´ v* rest
открывать *aht•krih•vaht´ v* open
открытка *aht•kriht•kah* postcard
открытый *aht•krih•tiy adj* open
отменять *aht•mee•nyat´* cancel (reservation)

отопление
ah•tahp•<u>lyeh</u>•nee•yeh heating

отпирать aht•pee•<u>raht</u>´ v unlock

отправляться
aht•prahv•<u>lyah</u>•tsah depart
(train, bus)

отпуск <u>ot</u>•poosk vocation
[holiday BE]

официант ah•fee•tsih•<u>ahnt</u>
waiter

очень <u>oh</u>•cheen´ very

очередь <u>oh</u>•chee•reet´ n queue

очки ahch•<u>kee</u> glasses (optical)

ошеломляющий ah•shih•
lahm•<u>lyah</u>•yoo•shcheey
stunning

ошибка ah•<u>shihp</u>•kah n mistake

П

пакет pah•<u>kyet</u> carton; packet

палата pah•<u>lah</u>•tah ward
(hospital)

палатка pah•<u>laht</u>•kah tent

палаточный лагерь
pah•<u>lah</u>•tahch•niy lah•geer´
campsite

палец <u>pah</u>•leets finger

палец ноги <u>pah</u>•leets nah•<u>gee</u>
toe

пальто pahl´•<u>toh</u> coat

панорама pah•nah•<u>rah</u>•mah
panorama

пара <u>pah</u>•rah pair

парацетамол
pah•rah•tsih•tah•<u>mol</u> acetaminophen [paracetamol BE]

парикмахер
pah•reek•<u>mah</u>•kheer
hairdresser

парк pahrk park

паром pah•<u>rom</u> ferry

паспорт pahs•pahrt passport

пассажирский класс
pah•sah•<u>zhihr</u>•skeey klahs
economy class

пациент pah•tsih•<u>yent</u> n patient

пачка сигарет <u>pahch</u>•kah
see•gah•<u>ryet</u> packet of
cigarettes

педикюр pee•dee•<u>kyoor</u>
pedicure

пелёнка pee•<u>lyon</u>•kah diaper
[nappy BE]

пепельница
<u>pyeh</u>•peel´•nee•tsah ashtray

перевес багажа pee•ree•<u>vyes</u>
bah•gah•<u>zhah</u> excess luggage

перевод pee•ree•<u>vot</u> translation

переводить pee•ree•vah•<u>deet</u>´
translate

переводчик pee•ree•<u>vot</u>•cheek
translator (text); interpreter
(speech)

перегреться
pee•ree•<u>gryeh</u>•tsah overheat

перед <u>pyeh</u>•reet before

переделывать
pee•ree•<u>dyeh</u>•lih•vaht´ alter

перекрёсток
pee•ree•<u>kryos</u>•tahk crossroad

перелом pee•ree•<u>lom</u> fracture
(of a bone)

переход pee•ree•<u>khot</u> pedestrian crossing

период pee•<u>ree</u>•aht period
(historical)

персонал peer•sah•<u>nahl</u> n staff

перчатка peer•<u>chaht</u>•kah glove

песок pee•<u>sok</u> sand

песчаный пляж pee•<u>shchah</u>•
niy plyahsh sandy beach

печатать pee•<u>chah</u>•taht´ v print

печень <u>pyeh</u>•cheen´ liver

пешеходная зона
pee•shih•<u>khod</u>•nah•yah
zoh•nah pedestrian zone
[precinct BE]

пешеходный маршрут
pee•shih•<u>khod</u>•niy
mahrsh•<u>root</u> walking route

пешком peesh•<u>kom</u> on foot

пещера pee•<u>shcheh</u>•rah cave

пикник peek•<u>neek</u> picnic

письмо pees´•<u>moh</u> letter

пить peet´ v drink

пиццерия pee•tsih•<u>ree</u>•yah
pizzeria

плавание <u>plah</u>•vah•nee•yeh
swimming

плавать <u>plah</u>•vaht´ swim

плавки <u>plahf</u>•kee swimming
trunks

план plahn n plan

пластырь <u>plahs</u>•tihr´ adhesive
bandage

плата <u>plah</u>•tah n charge

платина <u>plah</u>•tee•nah platinum

платить plah•<u>teet</u>´ v pay

платок plah•<u>tok</u> handkerchief

платформа plaht•<u>for</u>•mah n
track [platform BE]

платье <u>plaht</u>´•yeh dress

плащ plahshch raincoat

плёнка <u>plyon</u>•kah n film
(camera)

плечо plee•<u>choh</u> shoulder

плита plee•<u>tah</u> stove (cooker BE]

пломба <u>plom</u>•bah filling (dental)

плохой plah•<u>khoy</u> bad

пляж plyahsh beach

по делу pah <u>dyeh</u>•loo on
business

по крайней мере pah <u>kray</u>•neey
<u>myeh</u>•ryeh at least

по почте pah <u>poch</u>•tyeh by mail

побережье pah•bee•<u>ryezh</u>•yeh
coast

повар <u>poh</u>•vahr n cook

поворот pah•vah•<u>rot</u> n turning

повредить pah•vree•<u>deet</u>´ v
damage

повторять pahf•tah•<u>ryaht</u>´
v repeat

погода pah•<u>goh</u>•dah weather

под pahd under

подарок *pah•dah•rahk n* present (gift)

подвал *pahd•vahl* basement

подвозить *pahd•vah•zeet* give a lift

подержанный *pah•dyer•zhah•niy* second-hand

поднос *pahd•nos* tray

пододеяльник *pah•dah•dee•yahl'•neek* duvet

подозрительный *pah•dah•zree•teel'•niy* suspicious

подошва *pah•dosh•vah* sole (shoes)

подробности *pahd•rob•nahs•tee* details

подруга *pahd•roo•gah* girlfriend

подтвердить *paht•tveer•deet'* confirm (reservation)

подушка *pah•doosh•kah* pillow

поезд *poh•eest* train

поездка *pah•yest•kah* trip (journey)

пожар *pah•zhahr* fire

пожарная лестница *pah•zhahr•nah•yah lyes•nee•tsah* fire escape

позвоночник *pahz•vah•noch•neek* spine

поздний *poz•neey adj* late

пойти по магазинам *pie•tee pah mah•gah•zee•nahm* go shopping

пойти потанцевать *pie•tee pah•tahn•tsih•vaht'* go dancing

показывать *pah•kah•zih•vaht' v* show

покупать *pah•koo•paht'* buy

полный *pol•niy* full

половина *pah•lah•vee•nah* half

полотенце *pah•lah•tyen•tseh* towel

получать *pah•loo•chaht'* get (receive)

пользоваться *pol'•zah•vah•tsah v* use

помедленнее *pah•myed•lee•nee•yeh* slow down

поменьше *pah•myen'•sheh* smaller

помнить *pom•neet'* remember

помогать *pah•mah•gaht' v* help

понимать *pah•nee•maht'* understand

популярный *pah•poo•lyahr•niy* popular

поразительный *pah•rah•zee•teel'•niy* amazing

порез *pah•ryes n* cut (finger)

пороги *pah•roh•gee* rapids

порт *port* port (harbor)

портье *pahrt'•yeh* receptionist

посадочный талон *pah•sah•dahch•niy tah•lon* boarding card

посещать *pah•see•shchaht' v* visit

после *pos•lee* after (time/place)

последний *pahs•lyed•neey* last

посол *pah•sol* ambassador

посольство *pah•sol'•stvah* embassy

постельное бельё *pahs•tel'•nah•yeh beel'•yoh n* bedding

постричь *pah•streech v* trim (hair)

построенный *pah•stroh•yeh•niy* built

посуда *pah•soo•dah* crockery

посудомоечная машина *pah•soo•dah•moh•eech•nah•yah mah•shih•nah* dishwasher

посылать *pah•sih•laht'* send

посылка *pah•sihl•kah* package (mail)

потерять *pah•tee•ryaht' v* lose

потерять сознание *pah•tee•ryaht' sah•znah•nee•yeh v* collapse

потише *pah•tee•sheh* quieter

потому что *pah•tah•moo•shtah* because

похмелье *pahkh•myel'•yeh n* hangover

починить *pah•chee•neet' v* repair

почка *poch•kah* kidney

почта *poch•tah* post office

почта *poch•tah* mail (letters)

почти *pahch•tee* almost

почтовый ящик *pahch•toh•viy yah•shcheek* mailbox [postbox BE]

пошлина *posh•lee•nah* duty

правда *prahv•dah* true

правильный *prah•veel'•niy* right (correct)

православный *prah•vah•slahv•niy* Orthodox

прачечная *prah•cheech•nah•yah* laundro-mat [launderette BE]

превосходный *pree•vahs•khod•niy* superb

предлагать *preed•lah•gaht'* suggest

предприятие *preet•pree•yah•tee•yeh* company (business)

предъявлять *preed•yahv•lyaht'* declare

презерватив *pree•zeer•vah•teef* condom

преследовать *pree•slyeh•dah•vaht'* follow (pursue)

приблизительно *pree•blee•zee•teel'•nah* approximately

прибывать *pree•bih•vaht'* arrive

привлекательный *pree•vlee•kah•teel'•niy* attractive

приглашать _pree•glah•_<u>_shaht'_</u> invite

приглашение _pree•glah•_<u>_sheh_</u>_•nee•yeh_ invitation

приземляться _pree•zeem•_<u>_lyah_</u>_•tsah v_ land

примерочная _pree•_<u>_myeh_</u>_•rahch•nah•yah_ fitting room

принадлежать _pree•nahd•lee•_<u>_zhaht'_</u> belong

принадлежности _pree•nahd•_<u>_lyezh_</u>_•nah•stee_ accessories

принимать лекарство _pree•nee•_<u>_maht'_</u> _lee•_<u>_kahr_</u>_•stvah_ take medication

присмотр _pree•_<u>_smotr_</u> supervision

приходить _pree•khah•_<u>_deet'_</u> come

причудливый _pree•_<u>_chood_</u>_•lee•viy_ bizarre

приятный _pree•_<u>_yaht_</u>_•niy_ pleasant

пробор _prah•_<u>_bor_</u> parting (hair)

проверить _prah•_<u>_vyeh_</u>_•reet' v_ check (cheque BE)

провожать _prah•vah•_<u>_zhaht'_</u> accompany

прогноз погоды _prahg•_<u>_nos_</u> _pah•_<u>_goh_</u>_•dih_ weather forecast

программа _prah•_<u>_grah_</u>_•mah_ program

продавать _prah•dah•_<u>_vaht'_</u> sell

продавец _prah•dah•_<u>_vyets_</u> shop assistant

проездом _prah•_<u>_yez_</u>_•dahm_ in transit

проезжать _prah•eezh•_<u>_zhaht'_</u> _v_ pass

произносить _prah•eez•nah•_<u>_seet'_</u> pronounce

прокол _prah•_<u>_kol_</u> puncture

просить _prah•_<u>_seet'_</u> ask for

просматривать _prah•_<u>_smah_</u>_•tree•vaht' v_ browse

простуда _prah•_<u>_stoo_</u>_•dah_ cold; flu

простыня _prahs•tih•_<u>_nyah_</u> sheet (bedding)

протез _prah•_<u>_tes_</u> denture

противозачаточное средство _proh•tee•vah•_<u>_zah•chah_</u>_•ta hch•nah•yeh sryet•stvah n_ contraceptive

профессия _prah•_<u>_fyeh_</u>_•see•yah_ line (profession)

прыщ _prihshch_ acne

прямой _pryah•_<u>_moy_</u> _adj_ direct (train)

птица _ptee•tsah_ bird

пустой _poos•_<u>_toy_</u> empty

путеводитель _poo•tee•vah•_<u>_dee_</u>_•teel'_ guide book

пылесос _pih•lee•_<u>_sos_</u> vacuum cleaner

пьяный _pyah•_<u>_niy_</u> _adj_ drunk

Р

работа _rah•_<u>_boh_</u>_•tah_ job

работать _rah•_<u>_boh_</u>_•taht' v_ work

разбудить _rahz•boo•_<u>_deet'_</u> wake someone

разговаривать _rahz•gah•_<u>_vah_</u>_•ree•vaht' v_ talk

разговорник _rahz•gah•_<u>_vor_</u>_•neek_ phrasebook

размер _rahz•_<u>_myer_</u> size

район _rah•_<u>_yon_</u> region

ракетка _rah•_<u>_kyet_</u>_•kah_ racket (tennis)

раковина _rah•kah•vee•nah_ sink

рана _rah•nah n_ wound

ранний _rahn•niy_ early

раскладушка _rahs•klah•_<u>_doosh_</u>_•kah_ camp bed

расписание _rahs•pee•_<u>_sah_</u>_•nee•yeh n_ schedule (timetable BE)

рассвет _rahs•_<u>_vyet_</u> dawn

рассказывать _rahs•_<u>_kah_</u>_•zih•vaht'_ tell

растение _rahs•_<u>_tyeh_</u>_•nee•yeh n_ plant

растяжение _rahs•tee•_<u>_zheh_</u>_•nee•yeh n_ sprain

расчёска _rah•_<u>_shchos_</u>_•kah n_ comb

раунд _rah_<u>_•_</u>_oond_ round (of golf)

ребёнок _ree•_<u>_byoh_</u>_•nahk_ baby; child

ребро _reeb•_<u>_roh_</u> rib

регистрационная стойка _ree•gee•strah•tsih•_<u>_on_</u>_•nah•yah_ _stoy•kah_ check-in desk

регистрация _ree•gee•_<u>_strah_</u>_•tsih•yah_ reception (desk)

регистрироваться _ree•gees•_<u>_tree_</u>_•rah•vah•tsah_ _v_ check-in

рейс _reys_ flight

река _ree•_<u>_kah_</u> river

рекомендовать _ree•kah•meen•dah•_<u>_vaht'_</u> recommend

религия _ree•_<u>_lee_</u>_•gee•yah_ religion

ремень _ree•_<u>_myen_</u> belt

ремесла _ree•myos•_<u>_lah_</u> handicrafts

ремонт обуви _ree•_<u>_mont_</u> _oh•boo•vee_ shoe repair

рентген _reen•_<u>_gyen_</u> X-ray

ресторан _rees•tah•_<u>_rahn_</u> restaurant

рецепт _ree•_<u>_tsept_</u> prescription

родители _rah•_<u>_dee_</u>_•tee•lee_ parents

розетка _rah•_<u>_zyet_</u>_•kah_ electric outlet

романтичный
rah•mahn•teech•niy romantic

Россия *rah•see•yah* Russia

рост *rost* height

рот *rot* mouth

рубашка *roo•bahsh•kah* shirt

рубль' *roobl'* ruble [rouble]

рука *roo•kah* arm; hand

рукав *roo•kahf* sleeve

руководитель
roo•kah•vah•dee•teel' leader
(of group)

руководство *roo•kah•vod•stvah*
manual (car)

русский *roos•keey adj* Russian

русский язык *roos•keey*
yah•zihk Russian language

ручей *roo•chey n* stream

ручка *rooch•kah* pen

ручная кладь *rooch•nah•yah*
klaht' hand luggage

рыба *rih•bah* fish

рынок *rih•nahk* market

рюкзак *ryoog•zahk* rucksack

рядом *ryah•dahm* nearby

рядом с *ryah•dahm s* next to

С

с *s* with

с субтитрами *s*
soop•teet•rah•mee subtitled

сад *saht* garden

салфетка *sahl•fyet•kah* napkin

самолёт *sah•mah•lyot* plane

самообслуживание *sah•mah*
•ahp•sloo•zhih•vah•nee•yeh
self-service

сандалии *sahn•dah•lee*
sandals

сапоги *sah•pah•gee* boots

сауна *sah•oo•nah* sauna

сахар *sah•khahr* sugar

свадьба *svahd'•bah* wedding

свежий *svye•zhiy* fresh

свет *svyet n* light (electic)

светлый *svyet•liy adj* light
(opp. dark)

светофор *svee•tah•for* traffic
lights

свеча *svee•chah* candle

свидетельство
svee•dyeh•teel'•stvah
certificate

свитер *svee•teer* sweater

свободное время
svah•bod•nah•yeh vryeh•myah
free time

свободный *svah•bod•niy* available (unoccupied, free)

связаться *syah•zah•tsah v*
contact

сдача *zdah•chah* change (coins)

сейф *seyf n* safe (lock up)

секретарь *seek•ree•tahr'*
secretary

семья *seem'•yah n* family

сенная лихорадка
see•nah•yah
lee•khah•raht•kah hay fever

сердечный приступ
seer•dyech•niy prees•toop
heart attack

сердце *syer•tseh* heart

серебро *see•ree•broh n* silver

серый *syeh•riy* gray

серьги *syer'•gee* earrings

серьёзный *seer'•yoz•niy*
serious

сесть *syest'* sit

сигара *see•gah•rah* cigar

сигарета *see•gah•ryeh•tah*
cigarette

сильный *seel'•niy* strong
(potent)

симптомы *seemp•toh•mih*
symptoms

синагога *see•nah•goh•gah*
synagogue

синтетический *seen•teh•*
tee•chees•keey synthetic

синяк *see•nyahk* bruise

скала *skah•lah* cliff

скидка *skeet•kah* discount

сковорода *skah•vah•rah•dah*
frying pan

скорая помощь *skoh•rah•*
poh•mahshch ambulance

скоро *skoh•rah* soon

слева *slyeh•vah* on the left

следующий
slyeh•doo•yoo•shchey next

словарь *slah•vahr'* dictionary

сломан *sloh•mahn* broken

сломать *slah•maht' v* break

сломаться *slah•mah•tsah v*
break down (car)

служба *sloozh•bah n* service
(religious)

слуховой аппарат
sloo•khah•voy ah•pah•raht
hearing aid

слышать *slih•shaht'* hear

смеяться *smee•yah•tsah*
v laugh

смотровая площадка
smah•trah•vah•yah
plah•shchaht•kah overlook

снаряжение *snah•ree•zheh•*
nee•yeh equipment (sports)

снаряжение для дайвинга
snah•ree•zheh•nee•yeh dlyah
die•veen•gah diving equipment

снег *snyek n* snow

снотворное *snah•tvor•nah•yeh*
sleeping pill

собор *sah•bor* cathedral

событие *sah•bih•tee•yeh* event

совок *sah•vok* shovel

современный
sah•vree•myen•niy modern

современный танец
sah•vree•myen•niy tah•neets
contemporary dance

содержать *sah•deer•zhaht'*
contain

Соединенные Штаты _sah•ee•dee•nyoh•nih•ee shtah•tih_ United States

соленый _sah•lyoh•niy_ salty

солнечно _sol•neech•nah_ sunny

солнечные очки _sol•neech•nih•ee ahch•kee_ sunglasses

солнечный ожёг _sol•neech•niy ah•zhok_ sunburn

солнечный удар _sol•neech•niy oo•dahr_ sunstroke

сообщение _sah•ahp•shcheh•nee•yeh_ message

соска _sos•kah_ pacifier [soother BE]

сотрясение мозга _sah•tree•syeh•nee•yeh moz•gah_ concussion

спа _spah_ spa

спальный мешок _spahl'•niy mee•shok_ sleeping bag

спальня _spahl'•nyah_ bedroom

спасатель _spah•sah•teel'_ lifeguard

спасательная лодка _spah•sah•teel'•nah•yah lot•kah_ lifeboat

спасательный жилет _spah•sah•teel'•niy zhih•lyet_ lifejacket

спать _spaht'_ v sleep

специалист _spee•tsih•ah•leest_ specialist

спина _spee•nah_ back

спички _speech•kee_ matches

спорт _sport_ sport

спортзал _sport•zahl_ gym

спортклуб _sport•kloop_ sports club

спорттовары _spor•tah•vah•rih_ sporting goods store

справа _sprah•vah_ on the right

срочно _sroch•nah_ urgent

стадион _stah•dee•on_ stadium

стакан _stah•kahn_ glass

станция метро _stahn•tsih•yah meet•roh_ subway [underground BE] station

старый _stah•riy_ old

старый город _stah•riy goh•raht_ old town

статуя _stah•too•yah_ statue

стиль _steel'_ style

стиральная машина _stee•rahl'•nah•yah mah•shih•nah_ washing machine

стоимость _stoh•ee•mahst'_ value

столик _stoh•leek_ table

сторона _stah•rah•nah_ side (of road)

стоянка _stah•yahn•kah_ pitch (for camping)

стоянка такси _stah•yahn•kah tahk•see_ taxi stand [rank BE]

стоять в очереди _stah•yaht' v oh•chee•ree•dee_ stand in line

страна _strah•nah_ country (nation)

странный _strah•niy_ strange

страховка _strah•khof•kah_ insurance

стремянка _stree•myahn•kah_ ladder

стрижка _streesh•kah_ haircut

строить _stroh•eet'_ build

студент _stoo•dyent_ student

сувенир _soo•vee•neer_ souvenir

судороги _soo•dah•rah•gee_ cramps

сумка _soom•kah_ purse [handbag BE]

сумма _soo•mah_ amount

сухая стрижка _soo•khah•yah streesh•kah_ dry cut

счёт _shcot_ n bill

счёт за телефон _shcot zah tee•lee•fon_ telephone bill

США _seh sheh ah_ U.S.A.

сыпь _sihp'_ rash

сыро _sih•rah_ adj damp

Т

табак _tah•bahk_ tobacco

таблетка _tahb•lyet•kah_ pill (tablet)

также _tahk•zheh_ also

такси _tahk•see_ taxi

там _tahm_ there

таможенная декларация _tah•moh•zhih•nah•yah deek•lah•rah•tsih•yah_ customs declaration

таможня _tah•mozh•nyah_ customs

тампон _tahm•pon_ tampon

танец _tah•neets_ n dance (performance)

тапочки _tah•pahch•kee_ slippers

тарелка _tah•ryel•kah_ plate

театр _tee•ahtr_ theater

телевизор _tee•lee•vee•zahr_ TV-set

тележка _tee•lyesh•kah_ cart [trolley BE]

телефон _tee•lee•fon_ n phone

телефон-автомат _tee•lee•fon ahf•tah•maht_ pay phone

телефонный _справочник tee•lee•foh•niy sprah•vahch•neek_ directory (telephone)

тёмный _tyom•niy_ dark

температура _teem•pee•rah•too•rah_ temperature

теннис _teh•nees_ tennis

теннисные туфли _teh•nees•nih•ee toof•lee_ sneakers

теннисный корт _teh•nees•niy kort_ tennis court

тень _tyen'_ shade

тёплый _tyop•liy_ warm

термометр *teer•moh•meetr* thermometer

термос *ter•mahs* thermos flask

тесно *tyes•nah* crowded

тесный *tyes•niy* tight (loose)

течь *tych* v leak (roof, pipe)

типичный *tee•peech•niy* typical

тихий *tee•kheey* quiet

ткань *tkahn'* fabric (material)

толстый *tols•tiy* thick

тонкий *ton•keey* thin

тонуть *tah•noot'* drown

торговый центр *tahr•goh•viy tsentr* mall (shopping centre)

тот же самый *tot zheh sah•miy* same

трава *trah•vah* grass

традиционный *trah•dee• tsih•oh•niy* traditional

трамвай *trahm•vie* tram

трасса *trah•sah* trail (piste BE)

тратить *trah•teet'* spend

трейлер *trey•leer* caravan

тропинка *trah•peen•kah* path

трубка *troop•kah* pipe (smoking)

трудный *trood•niy* difficult

тряпка *tryahp•kah* dish cloth

туалет *too•ah•lyet* restroom (toilet BE)

туалетная бумага *too•ah•lyet•nah•yah boo•mah•gah* toilet paper

туман *too•mahn* fog

туннель *too•nel'* tunnel

турист *too•reest* tourist

туфли *toof•lee* shoes

тушь *toosh* mascara

ты *tih* you (informal)

тяжёлый *tee•zhoh•liy* heavy

У

угол *oo•gahl* corner

уголь *oo•gahl'* charcoal

удалять *oo•dah•lyaht'* extract (tooth)

удобства *oo•dops•tvah* facilities

удостоверение *oo•dah• stah•vee•ryeh•nee•yeh* identification

уезжать *oo•eezh•zhaht'* v leave

ужасный *oo•zhahs•niy* terrible

уже *oo•zheh* already

ужин *oo•zhih* dinner

узкий *oos•keey* narrow

укол *oo•kol* injection

Украина *oo•krah•ee•nah* Ukraine

укус *oo•koos* sting (wasp); bite (dog)

универсам *oo•nee•veer•sahm* supermarket

упаковочная пленка *oo•pah• koh•vahch•nah•yah plyon•kah* plastic wrap (cling film BE)

упаковывать *oo•pah•koh•vih•vaht'* v pack

урок *oo•rok* lesson

успокаивающее *oos•pah•k ah•ee•vah•yoo•shchee•yeh* sedative

усталый *oos•tah•liy* tired

утюг *oo•tyook* n iron

ухо *oo•khah* ear

уходить *oo•khah•deet'* go away

учитель *oo•chee•teel'* teacher

Ф

факс *fahks* n fax

фамилия *fah•mee•lee•yah* surname

фен *fyen* blow-dry

ферма *fyer•mah* farm

фильм *feel'm* movie (film BE)

фильтр *feel'tr* filter

фойе *fei•yeh* foyer (hotel, theater)

фольга *fahl'•gah* aluminium foil

фонтан *fahn•tahn* fountain

форма *for•mah* uniform

фотоаппарат

foh•tah•ah•pah•raht camera

фотография *fah•tah• grah•fee•yah* photograph

фраза *frah•zah* phrase

фунт *foont* pound (sterling)

футбол *food•bol* soccer (football BE)

Х

химчистка *kheem•cheest•kah* dry cleaner

хобби *khoh•bee* hobby (pastime)

холм *kholm* hill

холодильник *khah•lah• deel'•neek* refrigerator

холодный *khah•lod•niy adj* cold

холост *khoh•lahst* single (unmarried)

хороший *khah•roh•shiy* good

хотеть *khah•tet'* want

хрусталь *khroos•tahl'* n crystal

хрустальная посуда *khroos•tahl'•nah•yah pah•soo•dah* cut glass

художественный салон *khoo•doh•zhes•tvee•niy sah•lon* craft shop

Ц

цвет *tsvyet* color

цветок *tsvee•tok* flower

цветочный магазин *tsvye•toch•niy mah•gah•zeen* florist

целовать *tsih•lah•vaht'* v kiss

цель *tsel'* purpose

ценный *tseh•niy* valuable

центр (города) *tsentr (goh•rah•dah)* center (of town)

центральное отопление *tsihn•trahl'•nah•yeh ah•tahp•lyeh•nee•yeh* central heating

цепочка *tsih•poch•kah* chain

церковь *tser•kahf'* church

Ч

чайная ложка _chie•nah•yah losh•kah_ teaspoon
чайник _chie•neek_ kettle
чартерный рейс _chahr•ter•niy reys_ charter flight
час _chahs_ hour
час пик _chahs peek_ rush hour
часто _chahs•tah_ often
часы _chah•sih_ clock (watch)
часы посещений _chah•sih pah•see•shcheh•neey_ visiting hours
часы работы _chah•sih rah•boh•tih_ opening hours
чашка _chahsh•kah_ cup
чек _chek_ receipt
челюсть _cheh•lyoost'_ jaw
через _cheh•rees_ across
чистить _chees•teet' v_ clean
чистка лица _cheest•kah lee•tsah_ facial
чистый _chees•tiy adj_ clean
читать _chee•taht'_ read
что-то _shtoh•tah_ something
чулки _chool•kee_ stockings

Ш

шампунь _shahm•poon'_ shampoo
шапка _shahp•kah_ hat
шарф _shahrf_ scarf
шахматы _shahkh•mah•tih_ chess
швабра _shvahb•rah_ mop
шезлонг _shez•lonk_ deck chair
шёлк _sholk_ silk
шерсть _sherst'_ wool
шея _sheh•yah_ neck
широкий _shih•roh•keey_ wide
шкаф _shkahf_ cupboard
шлем _shlyem_ helmet
шорты _shor•tih_ shorts
шоссе _shah•seh_ highway [motorway BE]
штепсель _shtep•seel' n_ plug
штопор _shtoh•pahr_ corkscrew
шторы _shtoh•rih_ blinds
шумный _shoom•niy_ noisy
шутка _shoot•kah n_ joke
щётка для волос _shchot•kah dlyah vah•los_ hair brush

Э

экскурсия _eks•koor•see•yah_ guided tour
экскурсовод _eeks•koor•sah•vot_ tour guide
экспресс _eks•pres_ express
электричество _eh•leek•tree•cheest•vah_ electricity
электронная почта _ee•leek•troh•nah•yah poch•tah_ e-mail
электронный билет _ee•leek•tron•niy bee•lyet_ e-ticket
электронный ключ _eh•leek•tron•niy klyooch_ key card
эмаль _ee•mahl'_ enamel
эпилептик _ee•pee•lyep•teek n_ epileptic
эскалатор _ees•kah•lah•tahr_ escalator
этаж _eh•tahsh_ floor (level)

Ю

юбка _yoop•kah_ skirt
ювелирный магазин _yoo•vee•leer•niy mah•gah•zeen_ jeweler

Я

я _yah_ I
яд _yaht_ poison
язва _yahz•vah_ ulcer
язык _yah•zihk_ tongue
языковые курсы _yah•zih•kah•vih•yeh koor•sih_ language course
ярлык _yahr•lihk n_ label
ясли _yahs•lee_ nursery
яхта _yahkh•tah_ yacht

INDEX

Berlitz pocket guide

ST PETERSBURG

Third Edition 2018

Editor: Helen Fanthorpe
Authors: Michele A. Berdy and Magdalena Helsztyńska-Stadnik
Head of Production: Rebeka Davies
Picture Editor: Tom Smyth
Cartography Update: Carte
Update Production: Apa Digital
Photography Credits: Anna Mockford & Nick Bonetti/Apa Publications 4MC, 5MC, 33, 48, 49, 55, 72, 82; Bigstock 39, 41, 46, 54, 57, 58, 64, 67, 71, 105; Corbis 17, 18, 87, 89; Dreamstime 69; Fotolia 61, 78, 102; Getty Images 1, 6R, 21, 23, 45, 99; iStock 4TC, 4ML, 5T, 6L, 7, 12, 26, 30, 77, 79, 84, 91, 92, 95; Public domain 15; Shutterstock 4TL, 5TC, 5MC, 5M, 5M, 7R, 11, 29, 34, 37, 43, 50, 53, 62, 75, 80, 101
Cover Picture: iStock

Distribution
UK, Ireland and Europe: Apa Publications (UK) Ltd; sales@insightguides.com
United States and Canada: Ingram Publisher Services; ips@ingramcontent.com
Australia and New Zealand: Woodslane; info@woodslane.com.au
Southeast Asia: Apa Publications (SN) Pte; singaporeoffice@insightguides.com
Worldwide: Apa Publications (UK) Ltd; sales@insightguides.com

Special Sales, Content Licensing and CoPublishing
Insight Guides can be purchased in bulk quantities at discounted prices. We can create special editions, personalised jackets and corporate imprints tailored to your needs. sales@insightguides.com; www.insightguides.biz

All Rights Reserved
© 2018 Apa Digital (CH) AG and Apa Publications (UK) Ltd

Printed in China by CTPS

No part of this book may be reproduced, stored in a retrieval system or transmitted in any form or means electronic, mechanical, photocopying, recording or otherwise, without prior written permission from Apa Publications.

Contact us
Every effort has been made to provide accurate information in this publication, but changes are inevitable. The publisher cannot be responsible for any resulting loss, inconvenience or injury. We would appreciate it if readers would call our attention to any errors or outdated information. We also welcome your suggestions; please contact us at: berlitz@apaguide.co.uk
www.insightguides.com/berlitz

Berlitz Trademark Reg. U.S. Patent Office and other countries. Marca Registrada. Used under licence from the Berlitz Investment Corporation

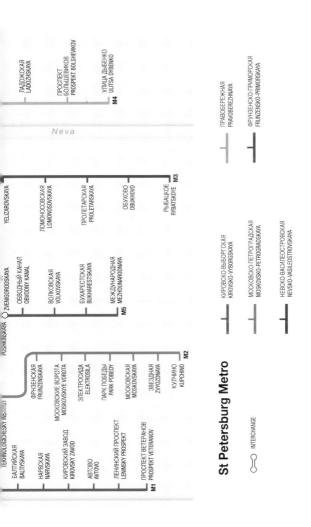

St Petersburg Metro

LADOZHSKAYA — ЛАДОЖСКАЯ
PROSPEKT BOLSHEVIKOV — ПРОСПЕКТ БОЛЬШЕВИКОВ
ULITSA DYBENKO — УЛИЦА ДЫБЕНКО
M4

Neva

YELIZAROVSKAYA
LOMONOSOVSKAYA — ЛОМОНОСОВСКАЯ
PROLETARSKAYA — ПРОЛЕТАРСКАЯ
OBUKHOVO — ОБУХОВО
RYBATSKOYE — РЫБАЦКОЕ
M3

ZVENIGORODSKAYA — ZVENIGORODSKAYA
OBVODNY KANAL — ОБВОДНЫЙ КАНАЛ
VOLKOVSKAYA — ВОЛКОВСКАЯ
BUKHARESTSKAYA — БУХАРЕСТСКАЯ
MEZHDUNARODNAYA — МЕЖДУНАРОДНАЯ
M5

PUSHKINSKAYA

TEKHNOLOGICHESKY INSTITUT

BALTIYSKAYA — БАЛТИЙСКАЯ
NARVSKAYA — НАРВСКАЯ
KIROVSKY ZAVOD — КИРОВСКИЙ ЗАВОД
AVTOVO — АВТОВО
LENINSKY PROSPEKT — ЛЕНИНСКИЙ ПРОСПЕКТ
PROSPEKT VETERANOV — ПРОСПЕКТ ВЕТЕРАНОВ
M1

FRUNZENSKAYA — ФРУНЗЕНСКАЯ
MOSKOVSKIYE VOROTA — МОСКОВСКИЕ ВОРОТА
ELEKTROSILA — ЭЛЕКТРОСИЛА
PARK POBEDY — ПАРК ПОБЕДЫ
MOSKOVSKAYA — МОСКОВСКАЯ
ZVYOZDNAYA — ЗВЁЗДНАЯ
KUPCHINO — КУПЧИНО
M2

◯—◯ INTERCHANGE

—|— KIROVSKO-VYBORGSKAYA
КИРОВСКО-ВЫБОРГСКАЯ

—|— MOSKOVSKO-PETROGRADSKAYA
МОСКОВСКО-ПЕТРОГРАДСКАЯ

—|— NEVSKO-VASILEOSTROVSKAYA
НЕВСКО-ВАСИЛЕОСТРОВСКАЯ

—|— PRAVOBEREZHNAYA
ПРАВОБЕРЕЖНАЯ

—|— FRUNZENSKO-PRIMORSKAYA
ФРУНЗЕНСКО-ПРИМОРСКАЯ

Berlitz®

speaking your language

phrase book & dictionary
phrase book & CD

Available in: Arabic, Brazilian Portuguese*, Burmese*, Cantonese Chinese, Croatian, Czech*, Danish*, Dutch, English, Filipino, Finnish*, French, German, Greek, Hebrew*, Hindi*, Hungarian*, Indonesian, Italian, Japanese, Korean, Latin American Spanish, Malay, Mandarin Chinese, Mexican Spanish, Norwegian, Polish, Portuguese, Romanian*, Russian, Spanish, Swedish, Thai, Turkish, Vietnamese
*Book only

www.berlitzpublishing.com